CONTENTS

A QUICK WORD WITH...
FRANK LAMPARD

England and Chelsea midfielder **Frank Lampard** is now in the veteran stages of his career – but he has no plans to hang up his boots just yet!

 FACT FILE

FRANK JAMES LAMPARD
Position: Midfielder
Birth date: June 20, 1978
Birth place: Romford, Essex
Height: 1.84m (6ft)
Clubs: West Ham, Swansea City (loan), Chelsea
International: England

YOU TURNED 33 IN 2011, WHAT'S IN STORE FOR THE FUTURE?

"I'm not thinking about the end, 33 is not what it was ten years ago. If you have the right manager you approach things differently and can carry on playing, hopefully I can perform well into my 30s. If you are a professional and you go about your job right you should be able to play until your 36 or 37 easily. I don't feel creaky when I am sat in the dressing room."

HOW DO YOU FEEL WHEN YOU LOOK BACK AT YOUR CAREER AT CHELSEA?

"I have a lot of pride and never expected to play as many games here, and not in ten years. I like to think I have a few years left in me yet."

AND PLAYING FOR YOUR COUNTRY?

"My appetite for England is as great as ever and it always will be until the day they don't want me or the day it becomes clear I'm not good enough anymore. Some people talk about retiring, I think about how many more years can I play. Everyone has seen the rise of the Premier League and the Champions League but it will always be a huge honour to play for your country."

HOW MUCH DOES IT HURT WHEN YOU LOSE A BIG MATCH?

"When you have played for as long as I have you understand that you can't win everything, but there's no point being negative or crying about it. The bad memories spur you on. There's nothing worse than the feeling you get losing a Champions League Final or semi-final."

WHEN YOU DO EVENTUALLY QUIT, ANY PLANS?

"I would like to get my badges and then see what happens. If you've played at the highest level you must have something and we have to try and get more English coaches in the future."

EXTRA TIME: Chelsea's record appearance maker is Ron 'Chopper' Harris. Between 1961 and 1980 the hardman defender turned out 795 times for the Blues. He has a hospitality suite named after him at Stamford Bridge.

CHELSEA FOOTBALL CLUB

DID YOU KNOW

- Lamps made his Chelsea debut on August 19, 2001 after moving from West Ham for £11m.

- Lamps has won more international caps whilst playing for the Chelsea than any other Blues player.

- Lamps has now played more than 500 games for the Blues – a mark he past shortly before the end of 2010-11 – making him the club's fourth-highest appearance maker.

- He has twice been Chelsea's Player of the Year.

EXTRA TIME: Chelsea's record goalscorer is Bobby Tambling with 202 between 1959 and 1970. At the end of season 2010-11, Lampard had 170 goals and was third in the Blues' goals list behind Kerry Dixon, who hit 193 between 1983 and 1992.

SHOOT ANNUAL 2012 **5**

FOCUS ON...

JACK WILSHERE
England's potential new captain...

FACT FILE

JACK ANDREW GARRY WILSHERE
Position: Midfielder
Birth date: January 1, 1982
Birth place: Stevenage, Hertfordshire
Height: 1.7m (5ft 7in)
Clubs: Arsenal
International: England

JACK WILSHERE HAS BEEN HAILED AS THE FUTURE OF ENGLAND BY A HOST OF MANAGERS AND FELLOW PROFESSIONALS. AND HE'S GOT DEFINITE VIEWS ON HOW HE WANTS TO PLAY FOOTBALL.

WILSHERE ON...

BREAKING THROUGH AT ARSENAL

"I always believed I could become an established part of the team but maybe I didn't think it would come this early. I have to thank the boss for showing faith in me and keeping me in there."

PROGRESSING HIS CAREER

"There is a lot more to come from me, especially at my age. There are players around I can learn from day-in and day-out. Playing with Cesc Fabregas and watching him go forward you can only learn."

HIS OWN GAME

"I like to get further forward but if it helps the team for me to sit then it is good for us. We have got quality strikers at Arsenal with the likes of Robin van Persie and others, so we will get goals. Teams come to the Emirates Stadium and they are scared and want to defend."

THE BOSS'S VIEW
ARSENE WENGER ARSENAL

"Jack is a talented player who can defend and attack. He defends well, he attacks well, he creates. He is a very confident lad but he has a hesitation some time to shoot himself and chooses to always give the ball. He is an outstanding player already with a lot more to come."

⑦ WILSHERE WONDERS

1. Jack joined Arsenal when he was just nine-years-old and made his reserve team debut at the age of 16.

2. Like fellow England hopeful Ashley Young, and former F1 champion Lewis Hamilton, he was born and raised in Stevenage, Hertfordshire.

3. He became the Gunners' youngest-ever player in September 2008 when he came on at Blackburn Rovers at the age of 16 years and 256 days.

4. Jack has never forgotten how Bolton's Owen Coyle had faith in him on loan – and has been back to watch the team.

5. He was Arsenal's Player of the Month for September 2010.

6. Jack became England's tenth youngest debutant when he appeared as a sub against Hungary in August 2010.

7. Jack appeared 14 times for Bolton Wanderers after joining them on loan in January 2011 for the rest of the season.

EXTRA TIME: Wilshere was the first 16-year-old to appear in the Champions League. He has also represented England at Under-16, 17, 19 and 21 levels as well as appearing for the full senior side.

THE BOSS'S VIEW
HARRY REDKNAPP TOTTENHAM

"I have never worked with a more single-minded goalscorer than Defoe I think he can actually score more goals than he does. He should get 20-plus every year. I still think there's part of his game he can improve. Jermain's goalscoring is fantastic and his movement too. But to be the complete frontman, his hold-up play can be better."

⚽ FACT FILE

JERMAIN DEFOE
Position: Striker
Birth date: October 7, 1982
Birth place: Beckton, East London
Height: 1.69m (5ft 7in)
Clubs: West Ham, Bournemouth (loan), Tottenham, Portsmouth, Tottenham
International: England

A NATURAL GOAL-SCORER, JERMAIN DEFOE WILL SHOOT ON SIGHT IF HE SPOTS THE SLIGHTEST OPENING ON GOAL. EQUALLY EFFECTIVE INSIDE OR OUTSIDE THE AREA HE'S A LETHAL WEAPON.

DEFOE ON...

TAKING PENALTIES

"If you practise enough, when you do take a penalty you'll be confident and if you are confident you will score. Most of it is in the mind. All penalties are big ones, even the ones in training because all of the lads are watching. You want to score and put pressure on yourself to score."

GOING 323 DAYS WITHOUT A GOAL

"I knew at the end of the day what to do out on the pitch, to keep getting in those scoring positions, that kept me going. I always believe things happen for a reason and that's why I will keep getting in the box."

GOAL-GRABBING

"As a forward it's important to get the goals, although I have always said if you don't score it's not the end of the world. You will get chances."

⑦ DEFOE WONDERS

1. Defoe missed out on Euro 2004 and World Cup 2006.

2. Defoe's cousin, Anthony Edgar, is a midfielder at West Ham. And just like JD, he has been out on loan to Bournemouth.

3. Defoe (5ft 7in) and Peter Crouch (6ft 7in) have been the little and large strike partnership for England, Portsmouth and Tottenham.

4. He made his England debut way back in March 2004, a 1-0 friendly defeat in Sweden.

5. The striker practises his finishing all of the time during training and admits he even gets a buzz from scoring in practise games.

6. Defoe made history when he was loaned to Bournemouth and scored in ten games in a row, and hit a total of 18 in 29 games.

7. Harry Redknapp managed Defoe at West Ham; bought him for Portsmouth, then took him back to Tottenham!

JERMAIN DEFOE
The livewire England striker

EXTRA TIME: Defoe scored a hat-trick for England in the 4-0 Euro 2012 qualifying victory over Bulgaria, at Wembley in September 2010. It was the first triple by a Three Lions player at the new Stadium. The other goal came from Adam Johnson.

DREAM TEAM

It's a side fans created from the best players to ever appear in the FA Cup Final. First, the keepers, defenders, midfielders, strikers, managers and dream players nominated...

GOALKEEPERS

Peter Schmeichel	David Seaman
Jim Montgomery	Dave Beasant
Bruce Grobbelaar	Bert Trautman
Gary Bailey	Neville Southall
Ray Clemence	Petr Cech

DEFENDERS

Ashley Cole	Ron Harris
Gary Pallister	Kevin Ratcliffe
Tony Adams	Jack Charlton
Frank McLintock	Steve Perryman
Gary Mabbutt	Bobby Moore

MIDFIELDERS

Roy Keane	Patrick Vieira
Ryan Giggs	Glenn Hoddle
Bryan Robson	Steven Gerrard
Liam Brady	John Giles
Stanley Matthews	Trevor Brooking

STRIKERS

Ian Rush	Jimmy Greaves
Jackie Milburn	Didier Drogba
Mark Hughes	Stan Mortensen
Nat Lofthouse	Michael Owen
Eric Cantona	Ian Wright

MANAGERS

Sir Alex Ferguson	Arsene Wenger	Bill Nicholson	Keith Burkinshaw	Sir Matt Busby
Kenny Dalglish	Ron Atkinson	Terry Neill	Bob Stokoe	Herbert Chapman

DREAM PLAYER

Peter Schmeichel	Ian Rush	Mark Hughes	Stanley Matthews	Bryan Robson
Eric Cantona	Glenn Hoddle	Tony Adams	Roy Keane	Ashley Cole

EXTRA TIME: The first-ever FA Cup Final was played at Kennington Oval in 1872. The Wanderers beat the Royal Engineers 1-0. The first final at Wembley was in 1923 when Bolton beat West Ham United 2-0.

AND THE WINNERS ARE...

PETER SCHMEICHEL

GARY PALLISTER   TONY ADAMS   BOBBY MOORE   ASHLEY COLE

STEVEN GERRARD   PATRICK VIEIRA   ROY KEANE   RYAN GIGGS

DREAM PLAYER

ERIC CANTONA   IAN RUSH

MANAGER
SIR ALEX FERGUSON

Tens of thousands of fans voted online in the ESPNsoccernet Cup of Dreams poll, to celebrate its first season broadcasting the FA Cup.

The ultimate FA Cup XI was selected from a list of 40 players nominated by ESPNsoccernet's editorial team as finalists. The players with the most votes in each position were named in the Ultimate XI

With the third-highest vote total, Ashley Cole's FA Cup record of six final wins saw him in the Ultimate XI's defence. Ryan Giggs received the most total votes.

Ian Rush, selected as one of the strikers, said: *"In the FA Cup you can get amateurs playing against the top players in the world. And that's what it is all about. For me it will always be something special. It is the most famous cup in the world. I didn't dream about the winning the league, I dreamt about playing in the FA Cup Final."*

Sir Alex Ferguson, admitted: *"My most vivid [FA Cup] memory was the Matthews final [the 1953 FA Cup Final, between Blackpool and Bolton Wanderers, with Blackpool winning 4-3]. Everyone in Scotland was rooting for Stanley Matthews. The Cup Final always had a special significance. Its a great cup."*

ESPN's live TV coverage of the FA Cup is led by Ray Stubbs with commentator Jon Champion and reporter Rebecca Lowe live from the games. From a custom-built set, coverage comes live from the game, capturing the environment and adding a new dimension to broadcasts.

ESPNHD

1963

He'd just scored a hat-trick for St. Johnstone against Rangers. He would later become much more famous as a manager.

Forget the dodgy hair... concentrate on the nose. It's why he's often called Pinnochio by opposition fans!

1979

FAMOUS FACES

Can you recognise these top football personalities from their rather old pictures? We've given you the year in which they were taken and a few clues. You could be amazed at who some of them are...

1980

There's no facial hair nowadays but this big, burly defender, has built himself a respectable record as a manager.

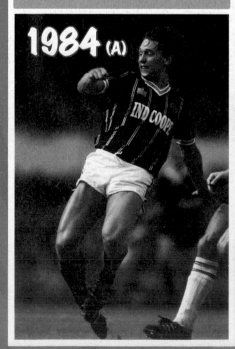

Here are a few clues: crisps, Match of the Day, goals galore...

1984 (A)

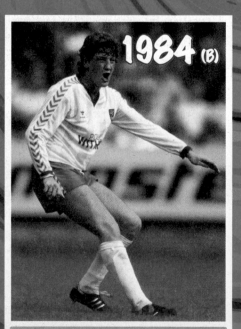

1984 (B)

He was turning out for Norwich, having left Gillingham but was to win England's top-flight with another team.

EXTRA TIME: When Sir Alex Ferguson picked up the Premier League trophy at the end of season 2010-11 it meant he had lifted 47 pieces of silverware. That includes 12 of the 19 top-flight titles won by Manchester United.

1992 (A)

His teams included Bournemouth, Liverpool, Tottenham and Southampton and his dad is a top manager!

1992 (B)

The stripes are not so familiar as his goal tally – a record for the Premier League which is unlikely to be broken… ever!

1997

A double whammy for you here! Boss and deputy boss at Bradford City – one later became a Premier League and Championship boss, the other a famous face on Sky Sports

1963	1984 (B)
1979	1992 (A)
1980	1992 (B)
1984 (A)	1997

EXTRA TIME: The English Premier League kicked off in season 1992-93. Leeds United were the last team to win England's top-flight – then known as Division One – before the formation of the new competition. Their manager was Howard Wilkinson.

FANTASTIC FOOTIE QUIZ

So what do you know about the stars of our favourite game? Let's find out!

Answers page 78.
No cheating – one point
for every correct answer.

1. Which Arsenal player arrived on a free from Bordeaux in summer 2010?

2. For which country do Man City's footballing brothers Yaya and Kolo Toure play for?

3. How much did Spain striker Fernando Torres cost Chelsea?

4. From which side did Tottenham sign Holland midfielder Rafael van der Vaart?

5. Striker Bobby Zamora has played for three Premier League sides, name two of them.

PART 1: PLAYERS

6. Asamoah Gyan was Sunderland's record buy at £13m after making his name at the 2010 World Cup with which country?

7. How did Everton midfielder Tim Cahill make World Cup history with Australia?

8. With which London club did England midfielder Scott Parker start his career?

9. Holland forward Dirk Kuyt joined Liverpool in 2006 from which Dutch side?

10. What nationality is Aston Villa midfielder Stiliyan Petrov?

11. Nationality of Newcastle's Hatem Ben Arfa.

12. Home country of Chelsea's David Luiz and Ramires.

SPOT THE BOSS!

Six top managers are on a scouting mission – watching one of the most promising young players in football. But they don't want to be spotted by club officials so they bought a ticket and disappeared into the crowd.

Can you find them hidden among the fans? Answers page 78.

EXTRA TIME: Harry Redknapp played at West Ham, Bournemouth and Brentford. He has managed the first two of those sides, plus Portsmouth, Southampton and Tottenham. Son Jamie played for Bournemouth, Tottenham and Southampton.

Here are the six bosses Shoot knows were at the game:

Sir Alex Ferguson **Steve Bruce** **Kenny Dalglish**
Harry Redknapp **Jose Mourinho** **Roberto Mancini**

GREATEST GAMES

The Premier League is often claimed to be the best in the world. Here are ten reasons why...

MAN UNITED 9 IPSWICH TOWN 0
MARCH 1995

Andy Cole became the first player to score FIVE in a Premiership game as United knocked up a record score for the competition.

LIVERPOOL 4 NEWCASTLE 3
MARCH 1997

It couldn't happen again – but it did! Three down at the break, Newcastle got it back to 3-3 before Robbie Fowler's 90th-minute winner.

LIVERPOOL 4 NEWCASTLE 3
APRIL 1996

Arguably the best-ever Premier League game. Even stunned Newcastle fans admit it was special. Stan Collymore scored the winner in the dying seconds.

TOTTENHAM 3 MAN UNITED 5
SEPTEMBER 2001

Spurs were 3-0 up at half-time. Andy Cole started the fight-back and David Beckham ended it with a 20-yard shot.

TOTTENHAM 4 ARSENAL 5
NOVEMBER 2004

Spurs scored first but after the hour were 3-1 down. Jermain Defoe got it to 3-2, Freddie Ljungberg made it 4-2, Ledley King replied for 4-3. Robert Pires scored a fifth for the Gunners and Kanoute got Tottenham's fourth.

EXTRA TIME: At the end of 2010-11 a total of 229 hat-tricks had been scored in the Premier League. Frenchman Eric Cantona got the first, for Leeds United, in a 5-0 victory over Tottenham in August 1992.

PORTSMOUTH 7
READING 4
SEPTEMBER 2007

Pompey were 2-0 up at half-time but by 48 minutes it was 2-2. It then went 5-2 with Benjani on a hat-trick. Reading snatched one back, but Pompey made it 6-3. In the last minute, Murty got his side's fourth before a Muntari penalty.

TOTTENHAM 4
ASTON VILLA 4
OCTOBER 2007

An hour gone and Villa were 4-1 up at White Hart Lane, despite the home side scoring first. Spurs pulled another back, got a penalty and, with seconds remaining, Younes Kaboul got the equaliser.

TOTTENHAM 6
READING 4
DECEMBER 2007

Spurs opened the scoring then went 2-1 down. They equalised but Reading struck back. Reading got it to 4-2 before Tottenham went on a goal spree that included a Berbatov hat-trick.

LIVERPOOL 4
ARSENAL 4
APRIL 2009

Four goals from Andrey Arshavin made it a Gunners night to remember at Anfield. Only an injury-time strike from Yossi Benayoun ensured a point apiece.

NEWCASTLE 4
ARSENAL 4
FEBRUARY 2011

Two down after three minutes, the home side were 4-0 adrift at half-time. The Geordies became the first Premier League team to come back from four down.

EXTRA TIME: Three players had totalled a record of eight red cards each in the Premier League by the time the competition reached the end of season 2010-11. They were defender Richard Dunne, striker Duncan Ferguson and midfielder Patrick Vieira.

FOCUS ON...

ADAM JOHNSON
Manchester City's tricky England winger

FACT FILE

ADAM JOHNSON
Position: Winger
Birth date: July 14, 1987
Birth place: Sunderland
Height: 1.75m (5ft 9in)
Clubs:
Middlesbrough, Leeds (loan), Watford (loan), Manchester City
International: England

HE'S FAST, HE'S SKILFUL, HE CAN SCORE GOALS AND DELIVER PIN-POINT CROSSES – THAT'S WHY ADAM JOHNSON HAS BEEN LIKENED TO THE GREAT RYAN GIGGS!

JOHNSON ON...

HIS BEST POSITION

"I'm left footed but when I was growing up as a winger you can play on either side. It's not really that different. I don't mind which side I play on. I actually do my best work down the right. I just play my own game. All top wingers play on opposite sides to they can come inside on their stronger foot."

HIS FAVOURITE WINGERS

"As a lad I liked Ryan Giggs and David Ginola in his prime – he used to go past people fully, not just half a yard to get a cross in. Apart from Arjen Robben, Lionel Messi and Franck Ribery not many go past people any more."

HIS AIMS

"I want to impress and excite the fans. That's the type of player I used to watch, people who attack, are skilful and take others on. I have to keep on playing well for my club and hopefully I'll be in every game for England."

THE BOSS'S VIEW
ROBERTO MANCINI MAN CITY

"He can play on the left and the right and can also play behind the main striker. He can continue to grow and I think he can be a very important player for this club. Adam can have a top career but has to understand he must work. I remember Ryan Giggs when he was young and the way he moved. Johnson is the same."

7 JOHNSON WONDERS

1. Born in Sunderland, Johnson supported their rivals Newcastle as a boy, but signed his first professional contract with another north east side, Middlesbrough!

2. When Man City played against Man United, Johnson wanted to grab the shirt from his idol Ryan Giggs, but was so disappointed to get beaten that he forgot!

3. After coming through Boro's famed academy, he got his first-team chance at the age of 18, his path to the side was blocked by another England winger, Stewart Downing.

4. He scored two goals at Wembley – whilst playing a schoolboy event on the famous pitch!

5. He signed for Manchester City in January 2010 for £8m, although he would have been available free that summer when he was out of contract.

6. His first goal for City was a last gasp equaliser at Sunderland – which didn't go down well with his family who are Black Cats fans!

7. Johnson's first England goal came when he took to the pitch for the final 16 minutes of the victory against Bulgaria in September 2010. He'd only been on for nine minutes.

EXTRA TIME: Many football followers expected Johnson to join England at the 2010 World Cup finals but he failed to make the final 23-man squad. He said later that missing out made him even more determined to play well and improve his game.

THE BOSS'S VIEW
SIR ALEX FERGUSON MAN UNITED

"Vidic has been a fantastic performer for us. We had to choose someone [as captain] we felt was going to be fit and playing every week. That is difficult when you rotate the squad the way we do. We felt Vidic was closest to that. He is a defender and I always think they make better captains. Vidic is a marvellous centre-back. Nemanja has courage and real determination."

⚽ FACT FILE

NEMANJA VIDIC
Position: Central defender
Birth date: October 21, 1981
Birth place:
Titovo Uzice, Yugoslavia
Height: 1.85m (6ft 1in)
Clubs: Red Star Belgrade, Spartak Subotica (loan), Spartak Moscow, Manchester United
International: Serbia

HE'S BEEN NICKNAMED THE SERBINATOR FOR HIS TOUGH-TACKLING. BUT NEMANJA VIDIC OFFERS LOTS MORE...

VIDIC ON...

HOW HE PLAYS

"I just try to do the best I can, to play my best in every game and in the end the fans and the media can form their own opinions."

IMPROVING HIS GAME

"Sometimes I read about people saying I had a hard time against a particular player but that makes me focus even more on doing my job properly. I always try to learn from my mistakes, to improve myself. I always want to improve, I am never happy, I always want to give more."

THE MANAGER

"Sir Alex always demands total concentration and a fighting approach. All of the players know their duties. Fergie has a special relationship with his players."

⑦ WONDERS OF VIDIC

1. He signed a new four-year deal at the start of season 2010-11 to try and end speculation about a transfer away from Old Trafford.

2. Vidic cost United £7m when he joined them from Spartak Moscow in January 2006.

3. When he arrived in England he could only speak a few words of English and learnt more from his team-mates and by watching television.

4. The defender took over as Man United captain at the start of the 2010-11 season because of the injury problems of his central defensive partner Rio Ferdinand.

5. He admits that he's taken a shine to eating fish and chips and the occasional bacon sarnie!

6. Vidic started his international career with the Yugoslav youth side, went on to play for Serbia and Montenegro and is now part of the Serbia side following independence.

7. A red card before the 2006 World Cup finals and then a training injury, meant he wasn't able to take part in Germany 2006.

NEMANJA VIDIC
Man United's tough tackling defender

EXTRA TIME: Vidic was the Barclays Premier League Player of the Season for 2008-09 and 2010-11. He was also in the PFA Premier League Team of the Season for 2006-07, 2007-08, 2008-09 and 2010-11.

SHOOT ANNUAL 2012 **19**

STAT ATTACK!

CHECK OUT SOME OF THESE FABULOUS FACTS AND STUNNING FIGURES

BANG!

116 mph

Experts reckon that Sheffield Wednesday striker David Hirst unleashed a shot against Arsenal that hit the crossbar at something like 186.6kmh (116mph) in season 1996-97. Good job he didn't hit the keeper!

When a match between Argentinos Juniors and Racing Club finished 2-2 the players had to take penalties to find out who would get an extra point, a rule in place in 1988. An amazing 44 penalties were taken before Argentinos won 20-19!

MARATHON!

HIGH SPEED PLAY!

Top-flight footballers perform a 15m sprint every 90 seconds.

The average time for a player in the Barclays Premier League to receive a pass and have played the next pass is just 1.15 seconds.

Of the 10km (6.2 miles) that an average player runs in a game more than 1km (1093.6 yards) will be done at top-speed.

The fastest players can reach speeds of 33 kmh (20.5mph) over longer sprint distances.

Losing the ball at the edge of your own penalty area can result in you picking the ball out of your own net in less than five seconds.

The longest-ever game of football took 35 hours and ended in a 333-293 score to All Stars against Cambray FC in Gloucestershire. The teams were raising cash for charity in 2010 and earned a place in the Guinness Book of Records.

EXTRA EXTRA TIME...

Turkey midfielder Hami Mandirali hit a free-kick against San Marino in 1997 that travelled at a staggering 266kmh (165mph).

WOOSH!

GOALS GALORE!

The biggest ever victory in a professional football match was Arbroath's 36-0 win against Bon Accord. It was a first round Scottish Cup game played in 1885. The game was 15-0 at half-time and the referee disallowed seven Arbroath goals for offside – later claiming they may not have been offside after all!

EXTRA TIME: Sheffield United's Brian Deane scored the Premier League's first-ever goal on August 15, 1992. It came after just five minutes on opening day and the striker added a penalty against Manchester United as the Blades won 2-1.

ONES TO WATCH!

Shoot pinpoints four young stars to keep an eye on over the next 12 months

DANIEL BOATENG

Position: Defender–Midfielder
Date of birth: September 2, 1992
Birth place: London
Gunners' fans have wanted a player like former captain Tony Adams to shore up their defence. Boateng might just be that player. He's got the skill, ability and strength that could push him into the Adams mode – but also has speed, which is something the former Arsenal skipper wasn't blessed with.

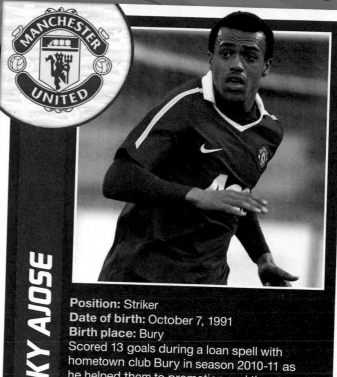

NICKY AJOSE

Position: Striker
Date of birth: October 7, 1991
Birth place: Bury
Scored 13 goals during a loan spell with hometown club Bury in season 2010-11 as he helped them to promotion and thrust himself into the spotlight. A creator as well as a scorer he can play central or wide and has pace. England Under-16 and 17 player.

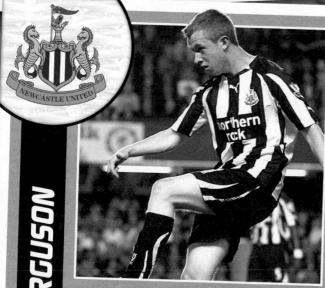

SHANE FERGUSON

Position: Left back–winger
Date of birth: July 12, 1991
Birth place: Derry, Northern Ireland
With a handful of first team appearances under his belt, Ferguson has proved to be a fast, tough tackling defender who isn't overawed by the reputations of much more seasoned pros. Although he has played for Northern Ireland in a friendly he is eligible and wanted by the Republic.

JOHN FLANAGAN

Position: Right back
Date of birth: January 1, 1993
Birth place: Liverpool
The teenager has broken through to the first team and already earned a reputation as a tough tackling defender who is also strong in the air. Although he knows his job is at the back, Flanagan also raids forward and can put over a decent cross. Winning massive praise from current and past Anfield heroes.

FANTASTIC FOOTIE QUIZ

So what do you know about the teams involved in our favourite game? Let's find out!

Answers page 78.
No cheating – one point for every correct answer.

1. Name the side who have played in the Premier League, Championship and League One at St. Mary's.

2. Which team plays at the Nou Camp?

3. What is the nickname of Stoke City?

4. Which is the second-biggest club ground in the Premier League?

5. Name the former European Champions who dropped down to League One.

PART 2: TEAMS

6. Who has won the most European Cups – Bayern Munich, Barcelona, Real Madrid or AC Milan?

7. Which English side has been the Champions of Europe the most number of times?

8. Who were the first team to win the FA Cup at the new Wembley?

9. Which Premier League team have a cockerel in their club badge?

10. Which two teams are nicknamed the Magpies?

11. Which Welsh side were the first in the Premier League?

12. Which Premier League side recorded just 11 points?

CAPTAIN'S CHOICE

Manchester United and England regular RIO FERDINAND gives his verdict on five of the best...

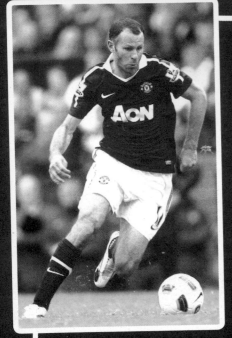

RYAN GIGGS
Man United

"He's probably one of the best players I've played with, if not the best. He will be appreciated more when he's retired. When we go abroad he's respected a lot more in foreign countries than in this country. When people throw names around saying someone's done this or done that for the Premier League, he very rarely gets mentioned. He's been the most successful footballer of our generation probably."

RAUL
Schalke and Spain

"Raul in the Champions League is one of the hardest I have had to play against. He doesn't play against you, he plays away from you. He asks you to come and mark him or let him hurt you with his passing."

NANI
Man United and Portugal

"He's the kind of player who gets me off my seat. He's exciting to watch and he always wants to beat his man, which is a great trait in an attacker. He always wants the ball, he's determined and he scores regularly, too. I don't think he gets the plaudits he deserves. A lot of people overlook him."

CHRIS SMALLING
Man United and England

"Chris is willing to learn, he wants to learn, he's hungry. You can see the desire in him. I think he's taking everything in during training and getting his rewards in games. He is a great lad and an enthusiastic young professional as well."

PETER CROUCH
England

"Lots of players at international level don't know how to deal with him. He is a quality player who knows his strengths, and if we play to them, then we'll see a good performance from him. He can be very awkward to mark. He is so tall, so he is different from what you face most weeks in the Premier League. He has a much better touch than most people give him credit for, and he is a good striker of the ball."

CRAZY KEEPERS!

Those guys between the goalposts aren't always the sanest people on the pitch – in fact sometimes they are totally bonkers! **Check out these players...**

WOBBLY BRUCE

South African Bruce Grobbelaar, who played for a number of English clubs, but was a mainstay at Liverpool in the 1980s and 90s, could have been renamed Bruce Wobbler.

He wobbled his legs in the 1984 European Cup Final but it was enough to put off the spot-kick taker and helped the Reds to victory.

He once took out a fan who ran onto the pitch and held him for police. And he gave away a goal when he had the ball taken from him as he tried to dribble past the opposition outside of his own area.

CENI THE CENTURION

If you've got a keeper like Rogerio Ceni in your side it's like having an extra striker – he's got a century of goals to his credit!

The Brazilian, part of his country's World Cup-winning squad in 2002, hit the record books when he became the first shot-stopper on the planet to reach 100 goals.

He hit that magic mark with a 25-yard free-kick for Sao Paulo against Corinthians, which was his 56th from similar kicks.

He'd notched the rest of his goals from penalties and in one season scored 21 for Sao Paulo!

HOTTIE CHILAVERT

Paraguay keeper Jose Luis Chilavert played in Argentina, Spain, France and Uruguay as he notched 62 goals in 546 games between the sticks. He took penalties and free-kicks and even scored eight goals in international games and was voted World's Best Keeper on three occasions.

MAD MARCUS

Marcus Hahnemann, of Wolves, Fulham and Reading, likes nothing better than blasting shells out of his big collection of guns!

He's a bit of a crackshot who keeps his artillery back home in America – but you may also see him zooming around in cars he has souped up himself, or spot him backstage at a heavy metal gig.

SCORPION-MAN!

You've heard of Spider-man and Batman... meet Scorpion man, Colombian Rene Higuita!

Over the space of more than 300 games he scored 38 goals – but it wasn't his scoring prowess that got him dubbed as crazy. Higuita perfected the art of the Scorpion-kick where he would bring his legs up behind his back to clear away shots whilst still looking up the pitch – like a scorpion brings up its tail to sting.

FOCUS ON...

LUIS SUAREZ
Liverpool's classy Uruguay striker

FACT FILE

LUIS ALBERTO SUAREZ DIAZ
Position: Striker
Birth date: January 24, 1987
Birth place: Salto, Uruguay
Height: 1.81m (5ft 11in)
Clubs: Nacional, Groningen, Ajax, Liverpool
International: Uruguay

SCORING ON YOUR DEBUT ALWAYS HELPS TO WIN OVER THE FANS. HELPING LIVERPOOL BEAT BITTER RIVALS MANCHESTER UNITED WILL IMPRESS THEM EVEN MORE. LUIS SUAREZ DID BOTH!

SUAREZ ON...

KENNY DALGLISH

"He is a person who you respect after only a few minutes of conversation. He is a legend at this club and in this city, but I think it's very important to judge people as you see them rather than just what you hear. He has lived up to that legend in my eyes."

GETTING THE NO.7 SHIRT

"I hadn't realised its history when I asked for the number. Now I'm happy that I did – I now know about players like Dalglish and Kevin Keegan. I have seen some videos of Dalglish scoring for Liverpool. He was a great player."

HIS WORLD CUP 2010 HANDBALL

"I regret what happened but if you asked 1,000 footballers I believe they would tell you they would have done the same thing. We were fighting for a World Cup semi-final. I had the chance to stop a goal. I just did it."

THE BOSS'S VIEW

KENNY DALGLISH LIVERPOOL

"Suarez scored on his debut which is fantastic for him and great for the supporters. He's got a fantastic goalscoring record. He's scored goals for Ajax and at the World Cup, and is somebody I think will really excite the fans. He is a happy guy and has a smile on his face, a twinkle in his eye and there is mischief in there."

SUAREZ WONDERS

1. Liverpool boss Kenny Dalglish has made the striker feel welcome at Anfield by talking to him in Spanish as the player is only learning English.

2. Suarez was Liverpool's record signing for just over 90 minutes as the club signed striker Andy Carroll from Newcastle in the same evening.

3. When he was just ten, Suarez used to be Liverpool when he switched on his PlayStation.

4. The Reds paid Ajax £22m in the January 2011 transfer window to sign the Uruguayan.

5. Interest in Suarez was high after he hit 49 goals in 2010, including 35 in 33 Dutch League matches.

6. Like former Ajax players Johan Cruyff, Marco van Basten and Dennis Bergkamp, he scored more than 100 goals for the Amsterdam giants.

7. He has scored more than a goal every other game since starting his professional career in 2005.

EXTRA TIME: Suarez is not the first Uruguayan to play in England's top-flight. Others have included Gus Poyet (Chelsea and Tottenham), Diego Forlan (Man United), Walter Lopez (West Ham) and Walter Pandiani (Birmingham City).

THE CAPTAIN'S VIEW
JOHN TERRY CHELSEA

"David is a great lad to have around and a talent on the field. He will be a Chelsea legend. He is young and likes to enjoy training but it is important the fans know that on a match day he is very serious and focused. With his ability on the ball, he could step into midfield quite easily."

FACT FILE

DAVID LUIZ MOREIRA MARINHO
Position: Defender
Birth date: October 7, 1982
Birth place: Sao Paulo, Brazil
Height: 1.85m (6ft 1in)
Clubs: Vitoria, Benfica, Chelsea
International: Brazil

THE COOL, CALM AND CULTURED DEFENDING OF DAVID LUIZ WON OVER CHELSEA FANS WITHIN WEEKS OF HIS ARRIVAL AT CHELSEA. REGARDED AS JOHN TERRY'S EVENTUAL REPLACEMENT HE'S SIMPLY BRAZILIANT!

LUIZ ON...

JOINING CHELSEA

"It is much easier to settle in when the players, manager and fans help me. It's why I've got used to a new club so well. I am very happy because I am at one of the best teams in the world."

HIS BELIEFS

"I go to church, my religion is very important to me. I praise God and thank the Lord for my family, health and giving me my talent to play football. My faith gives me belief I can play, improve and get a lot better as a footballer."

THE PREMIER LEAGUE

"I chose to come here because it is the best in the world, a really tough league. I knew from watching TV that the Premier League is a lot more physical and faster than anything I played before. But it's not about adapting aspects of my game, it's about improving."

⑦ LUIZ WONDERS

1. Chelsea grabbed Luiz for £23m from Portuguese giants Benfica during the January 2011 transfer window.

2. Luiz's father, Ladislao, was a midfielder with Brazilian side Atletico Mineiro but packed in football at the age of 20 as he didn't get paid enough to support his family.

3. He scored goals against both Manchester City and United during his first few games for the Blues.

4. Chelsea team-mates nicknamed him Valderama after the Colombian midfielder with the same big hair style!

5. When he arrived at Stamford Bridge he was the reigning Portugal Player of the Year.

6. Luiz was just 14 when he left home to join Vitoria – with the aim of making it big so that he could support his whole family!

7. It took him just a few weeks to earn his first Barclays Player of the Month award, for March 2010.

DAVID LUIZ
Chelsea's cool-headed Brazil defender

EXTRA TIME: Luiz's arrival at Stamford Bridge was made easier by the fact that two fellow countrymen were already there – Brazil defender Alex, on the books at Chelsea since 2004, and midfielder Ramires who signed the previous summer.

SHOOT ANNUAL 2012   27

NAME THE PLAYERS!

Follow our clues and see if you can name the silhouette stars...

PLAYER A

PLAYER B

- My nickname is the same as a small vegetable!
- I was revealed as the fastest player at the 2010 World Cup finals.
- My current club bought me for just £6m and I scored 13 Premier League goals in my first season.
- My home country is noted for its chilli and Fajitas!
- My first game at South Africa 2010 was against the host country.

- I'm a midfielder who loves to get forward and score goals.
- I've got the best record for headed goals in the Premier League
- My club play in blue, my country in green and yellow.
- I scored my country's first-ever goals at a World Cup final.
- Millwall sold me for just £1.5m to my current club.

PLAYER C

PLAYER D

- In 2011 I became my country's youngest-ever captain.
- The previous year I was voted my country's Young Player of the Year.
- A broken leg kept me out of the game for nine months between February and November 2010.
- I was loaned to Nottingham Forest and Cardiff to regain fitness after my injury.
- My current club bought me for just under £5m when I was still only 17.

- I arrived in the Premier League during the January 2011 transfer window.
- My club forked out almost £23m to buy me from Amsterdam side Ajax.
- I scored on my debut, against Stoke City.
- My home country is in South America, where I began my career before a move to Holland with Groningen.
- I was once nicknamed 'Cannibal' for biting another player on the shoulder.

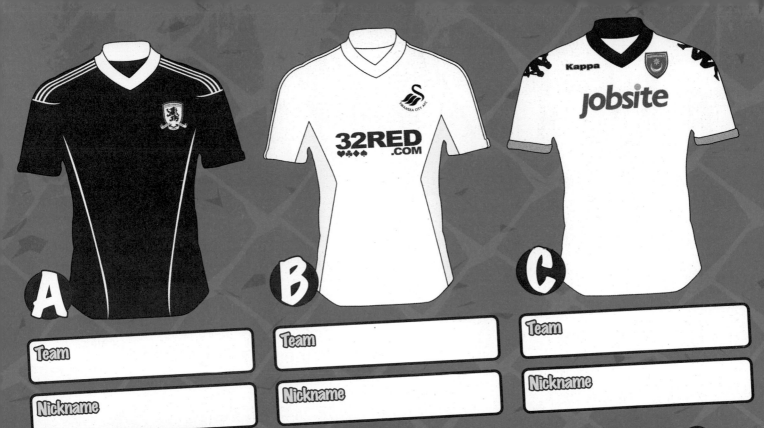

A

Team

Nickname

B

Team

Nickname

C

Team

Nickname

CHAMPIONSHIP CHALLENGE

It's one of the toughest leagues in the world – and the rewards for promotion from the Championship can be massive, with places in the Premier League at stake. We've printed images of six kits used by teams in England's second-flight in 2010-11 – but can you tell us which teams they are? There is a mixture of home and away kits, and to make it a little bit more difficult we also want you to give us the teams' nicknames!

D

Team

Nickname

E

Team

Nickname

F

Team

Nickname

OLLY DAYS!

Haven't you just got to love him?
Fellow Premier League gaffers reckoned Blackpool boss Ian Holloway was their 2010-11 Manager of the Season for his side's battling performances and despite relegation. Shoot reckons he is boss of the year for his sense of humour. Here's the world according to Olly…

Blowing Bubbles

"I don't normally swear towards women, ever since I did it to my mum when I was young and didn't know what the words meant. She had me eating a bar of soap and locked in my bedroom."

Being nice to female match officials…

Calling the shots

"We might as well have got a shotgun and blown off both of our feet."

After his side crashed 3-1 at home to Wigan…

Men in Black-pool

"We are like the Men in Black zapping the aliens together. Bosh! Zap!"

Ok, so he really lost it on this one…

EXTRA TIME: Before he went into management, Ian Holloway was a midfielder with Bristol Rovers, Wimbledon, Brentford, Torquay and Queen's Park Rangers. His first manager's job was with Bristol Rovers, who he had three spells with as a player.

My Town

"Where is Rimini? Would you find a donkey walking down the street there? Can you get a stick of rock there or have they got a big dipper?"

Standing up for 'Pool after it was compared to Rimini by Man City's Roberto Mancini…

Blackpool Rocks

"I'm being serious when I say we had thousands, not hundreds, of players recommended to us by agents. I feel like a gold prospector. One of them may be a lump of gold but most won't be."

Quite a few of his players proved to be the right type of nugget…

My Team

"I should be allowed to deal with them (my players) as I like, like I do with my children. They only get an ice cream if they deserve it. Mind you they are 20-years-old so they can buy their own."

When people questioned his team choice…

…and one of his players said!

"Every time he speaks he is like a preacher to me. Sometimes he quotes excerpts from the Bible."

Keeper Richard Kingson reveals Olly is god-like!

BAD HAIR DAYS!

Sometimes players should think twice before they give us an idea for a feature! Manchester United veteran Ryan Giggs admitted: "You do look back and cringe at your haircuts and some of the gear you used to wear." We did look back… start cringing Giggsy!

EXTRA TIME: Holloway made just over 700 appearances during his playing career between 1981 and 1999. He took on a player-manager role in 1996 and at the end of season 2010-11 he had been a boss in charge of 695 games!

SHOOT ANNUAL 2012 **31**

FOCUS ON...

TIM HOWARD
Everton's reliable shot-stopper

FACT FILE

TIMOTHY MATTHEW HOWARD
Position: Keeper
Birth date: March 6, 1979
Birth place: New Jersey, USA
Height: 1.91m (6ft 3in)
Clubs:
North Jersey Imperials, MetroStars,
Manchester United, Everton
International:
USA

TIM HOWARD HAS PROVED THAT THERE IS LIFE AFTER OLD TRAFFORD. DURING THE YEARS THAT MAN UNITED HAVE BEEN LOOKING FOR A NEW NO.1 KEEPER THE AMERICAN HAS MADE A NAME FOR HIMSELF AT EVERTON.

HOWARD ON...

HIS BOSSES
"I have had the good fortune of playing for Sir Alex and David Moyes. They are both fiery Scots who are entrenched in the mindset of not going anywhere. I feel that has been a huge benefit for me."

COPING WITH FAME
"There's always someone there with eyes on you or something to say. And the games mean so much to these people that they're always pointing a finger, good or bad. It's hard to get used to at first.

BEING AN EVERTONIAN
"Every club has history, but it's been branded as the people's club. For me this has become my home. If you're a hard worker, that you really care about the club, people will appreciate you."

THE BOSS'S VIEW
DAVID MOYES EVERTON

"Tim Howard is a professional who works very hard at his game. He has been extremely consistent in his years with us. He's not the kind of keeper that broods over a mistake, he gets his head down and does his work. He is a conscientious boy with his work."

 ## HOWARD WONDERS

1. He has passed the milestone of 300 league games in English football and has played more than 400 career games.

2. Howard was voted the Premier League's Goalkeeper of the Year in 2003, his first season at Man United, where he had replaced Fabien Barthez.

3. He went on loan to Everton for 2006-07 before making the move permanent at the end of that season for around £3m.

4. Howard won the Golden Glove as best keeper at the 2009 Confederations Cup where the USA were runners-up.

5. He was Man of the Match at World Cup 2010 when the USA held England to a draw.

6. The keeper was between the posts for 77 games during his three years at Manchester United – where he was replaced by Edwin van der Sar.

7. He was ever-present in the Premier League for Everton in 2008-09, 2009-10 and 2010-11. He holds the club record with 16 league clean sheets in a season.

EXTRA TIME: When Howard was asked to name his dream five-a-side team he put Everton team-mate Phil Jagielka in goal! Jags has played there before and likes to think he is a bit useful. Howard said he made his choice so he could sit out the game!

THE BOSS'S VIEW
PETER BEARDSLEY NEWCASTLE RESERVE TEAM BOSS

"He's obviously got ability, he's got that kind of attitude. He's a good lad and I have to be honest, he's an even better player than I thought he was. I knew he was good but now I think he's excellent."

THE LOAN STAR TURNED INTO A BARGAIN BUY WHEN HE MOVED TO NEWCASTLE – AND NOW HE'S BEING TIPPED FOR FULL ENGLAND HONOURS.

SIMPSON ON...

SIGNING FOR NEWCASTLE

"Everyone is passionate. There are 50,000 every week at St. James' and you know when you sign just what sort of a place you are at. It was the best time for me to leave United and get first-team football but I will never forget my time there. I have moved on and am still at a big club."

FORMER TEAM-MATES

"I signed for United when I was 11 and Roy [Keane] was one of my idols. He always gave 100 per cent and that is the type of player I want to be. I trained every day with the likes of Scholes, Giggs, Keane, Rooney and Ronaldo. Just watching those guys you learn from them."

MANAGERS

"Playing under Keane at Sunderland was great. I have learned from all my managers. I owe a lot to Chris Hughton. He got me in on loan at Newcastle and then signed me. Alan Pardew is honest and if he doesn't think you have done well he will tell in a constructive way."

(7) SIMPSON WONDERS

1. He joined Newcastle on a four-month loan and made the move permanent in the January 2010 transfer window for around £500,000.

2. Simpson won the Championship on loan at Sunderland in 2007 – and lifted the same trophy with Newcastle in 2010.

3. An injury gave the defender a chance to appear on Sky Sports Soccer AM programme in the middle of the season.

4. Simpson, Darron Gibson, Jonny Evans and Fraizer Campbell were all on loan at the same time from United to Belgian side Royal Antwerp.

5. Having played for both big north east sides, Simpson has stated categorically that he regards his current club as the biggest!

6. The defender wishes that he'd had the chance to meet pop legend Michael Jackson to talk about music.

7. After scoring his first goal of 2010-11 he reckoned it was all down to a fish pedicure – where tiny fish nibble dead flesh off your feet!

DANNY SIMPSON
Newcastle United's no-nonsense right back

EXTRA TIME: Simpson is still full of praise for Sir Alex Ferguson, who allowed him to leave Manchester United. The full back reckons Fergie will remain in charge at Old Trafford as long as his health permits – and that he still loves every goal United score.

SHOOT ANNUAL 2012 **33**

FANTASTIC FOOTIE QUIZ

So what do you remember about some of football's greatest games and fixtures? Let's find out!

Answers page 94. No cheating – one point for every correct answer.

1. You remember Spain won the 2010 World Cup Final – but who did they beat?

⚽

2. Who scored the winner in the above game?

⚽

3. Who scored Spain's winner against Germany in the final of Euro 2008?

⚽

4. Liverpool won the European Cup in Istanbul in 2005. What was the score after 90 minutes?

⚽

5. Who scored Chelsea's winning goal against Man United in the 2007 FA Cup Final at Wembley?

⚽

PART 3: GAMES

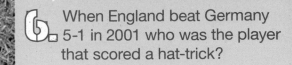

6. When England beat Germany 5-1 in 2001 who was the player that scored a hat-trick?

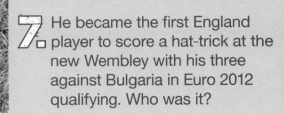

7. He became the first England player to score a hat-trick at the new Wembley with his three against Bulgaria in Euro 2012 qualifying. Who was it?

8. Match of the Day presenter Gary Lineker has scored five hat-tricks for England, including one in the 1986 World Cup finals. True or false?

9. Which team ended Arsenal's 49-game unbeaten run in the Premier League?

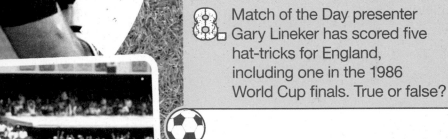

10. Manager of Blackburn Rovers when they won the Premier League in 1995?

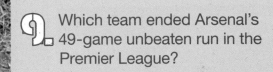

11. Newcastle, 0-4 down, made it 4-4 against which side?

12. Who equalised in England 2 Switzerland 2, June 2011?

TOP TEN LISTS

Goals, points, money – these are the best in the Premier League and world!

MOST POINTS

1.	Man United	1,574
2.	Arsenal	1,397
3.	Chelsea	1,338
4.	Liverpool	1,282
5.	Aston Villa	1,051
6.	Tottenham	1,017
7.	Everton	978
8.	Newcastle	952
9.	Blackburn	938
10.	West Ham	764

MOST APPEARANCES

1.	David James	573
2.	Ryan Giggs	573
3.	Gary Speed	535
4.	Sol Campbell	503
5.	Frank Lampard	491
6.	Emile Heskey	488
7.	Paul Scholes	465
8.	Jamie Carragher	463
9.	Phil Neville	460
10.	Alan Shearer	441

GOALS AT WORLD CUPS

1. Brazil	216	2. Germany	206	3. Italy	153	4. Argentina	124	5. England	97
6. Spain	96	7. France	86	8. Holland	76	9. Uruguay	66	10. Sweden	61

WORLD'S RICHEST CLUBS

1.	Real Madrid	£438.6m
2.	Barcelona	£398.1m
3.	Manchester United	£349.8m
4.	Bayern Munich	£323m
5.	Arsenal	£274.1m
6.	Chelsea	£255.9m
7.	AC Milan	£235.8m
8.	Liverpool	£225.3m
9.	Inter Milan	£224.8m
10.	Juventus	£205m

TOP SCORERS

1.	Alan Shearer	260
2.	Andy Cole	189
3.	Thierry Henry	174
4.	Robbie Fowler	163
5.	Les Ferdinand	149
6.	Michael Owen	148
7.	Teddy Sheringham	147
8.	Frank Lampard	135
9.	Jimmy Floyd Hasselbaink	127
10.	Dwight Yorke	123

FOOTBALL'S HIGHEST EARNERS

1.	Lionel Messi - *Barcelona*	£26.9m
2.	Cristiano Ronaldo - *Real Madrid*	£23.9m
3.	Wayne Rooney - *Man United*	£18m
4.	Kaka - *Real Madrid*	£16.7m
5.	David Beckham - *LA Galaxy*	£16.5m
6.	Ronaldinho - *Flamengo*	£15.9m
7.	Carlos Tevez - *Man City*	£13.4m
8.	Frank Lampard - *Chelsea*	£12.3m
9.	Yaya Toure - *Man City*	£11.9m
10.	Thierry Henry - *New York Red Bulls*	£11.5m

*CORRECT TO END OF SEASON 2010-11

CAPTAIN'S CHOICE

Chelsea and England skipper **JOHN TERRY** gives his verdict on five of the best...

LIONEL MESSI
Barcelona and Argentina

"He is so good – incredible and unplayable at times. If he comes inside at any time you need two men to double up on him. You can't get near him in a one-on-one. He is a special talent, especially when he is performing at the Nou Camp."

NICOLAS ANELKA
Chelsea and France

"Nico has stressed before how much he loves the club. The fans love him, the players love him and we would love him to stay here for years. He is a great character, a nice guy and a good professional, someone the young players can look up to and learn from."

JACK WILSHERE
Arsenal and England

"I played against him when he was on loan at Bolton a couple of years ago and for someone so small as well as the strength, he has the ability to glide past people, he has a great turn of pace, an amazing left foot and someone we're seeing game after game growing into a very good player. He has the ability to deal with the pressure and the confidence in himself and his quality."

FERNANDO TORRES
Chelsea and Spain

"We have had some great battles. I was very impressed when he made his debut against us and scored. He is one of the strongest out there. His pace is frightening, his heading unbelievable and his finishing top drawer."

WAYNE ROONEY
Manchester United and England

"Wayne has been different class. He has really matured as a player. Wayne is very talented and his potential is frightening. I was saying to him he could possibly get to 150 caps. It is a reachable target – and certainly 100."

WHICH BALL?

Our smart designer has used computer technology to create more balls in each action of the four action shots on these pages. It's your job to decide which is the real one in each picture and write your answers in the space provided. Answers page 78.

GAME ONE

GAME TWO

EXTRA TIME: Thierry Henry has been top scorer in the Premier League more times than any other player – taking the Golden Boot four times! Alan Shearer, the division's all-time record scorer, was top goal getter three times during his career.

GAME THREE

GAME FOUR

GAME ONE	Chelsea v Liverpool	The correct ball is:	
GAME TWO	Blackburn Rovers v West Ham	The correct ball is:	
GAME THREE	Chelsea v Manchester City	The correct ball is:	
GAME FOUR	Birmingham City v Arsenal	The correct ball is:	

EXTRA TIME: Harry Redknapp is the only Premier League boss to win the Manager of the Month award with four different top-class sides. He won with West Ham United, Portsmouth, Southampton and Tottenham.

PHIL BARDSLEY
Sunderland's tough tackling defender

FACT FILE

PHILLIP ANTHONY BARDSLEY
Position: Defender
Birth date: June 28, 1985
Birth place: Salford, Manchester
Height: 1.8m (5ft 11in)
Clubs: Manchester United, Royal Antwerp (loan), Burnley (loan), Rangers (loan), Aston Villa (loan), Sheffield United (loan), Sunderland
International: Scotland

PHIL BARDSLEY WAS SWEATING ON WHETHER HE WOULD GET A NEW CONTRACT AT THE STADIUM OF LIGHT. HIS BOSS WAS HOPING HE WOULDN'T GO! THE DEFENDER SIGNED ON UNTIL 2014.

BARDSLEY ON...

PRE-SEASON BOOT CAMP

"In the last two summers when I came back I felt most of the lads were ahead of me in terms of fitness. So I went to the gym and gave it a crack. I trained for two weeks and did treadmill and aerobics in the morning and ten rounds with the punchbag in the afternoon. Then I would do circuits. I have noticed the difference on the pitch."

SIR ALEX FERGUSON

"I still call him gaffer. It was tough leaving because I had been there since I was nine. I grew up there, lived there, breathed it, drank it. It's hard playing against them. I have to take the scarf off and leave it on the sidelines for 90 minutes."

CHOOSING SCOTLAND

"I don't have one regret whatsoever. I'm fully Scottish now and I'm here as long as the manager picks me."

THE BOSS'S VIEW
STEVE BRUCE SUNDERLAND

"Phil has done very, very well. He has played his part, he is a valuable member of the squad and he has been rewarded for that. He's somebody I wanted to have as part of my squad. I know the lad well; I've known him since he was a boy."

BARDSLEY WONDERS

1. Bardsley qualifies to play for Scotland because of his Glasgow-born father.

2. Former Sunderland manager and ex-Man United captain Roy Keane bought the defender from Old Trafford for £2m in 2008.

3. When he went on loan to Sheffield United his manager there was former Man United captain Bryan Robson.

4. It's not often he gets the chance, but when he can Bardsley will be seen in the stands supporting Manchester United – although when they play Sunderland he is a Black Cat through and through.

5. He was just eight-years-old when he joined the Red Devils' Academy and progressed through all of their ranks to the first-team, where he made eight Premier League appearances.

6. Bardsley was born just a short free-kick from United's old training ground, before it moved to Carrington.

7. Despite starting his career in 2003, it took him until January 2011 to score his first Premier League goal, the winner against Aston Villa.

EXTRA TIME: There's no shortage of familiar faces for Bardsley at Sunderland with former Man United players Kieran Richardson and Fraizer Campbell on the books, plus Danny Welbeck who was on loan from Old Trafford in 2010-11.

TEAM MATE'S VIEW
CRAIG GARDNER BIRMINGHAM CITY

"Ben is different class. He was been brilliant from day one for Birmingham. He is a great professional, different class, and he should be England's No.1. We paid £6m for him but he would have been a bargain at £20m. He is a top-class keeper and a top-class lad."

FACT FILE

BENJAMIN ANTHONY FOSTER
Position: Keeper
Birth date: April 3, 1983
Birth place:
Leamington Spa, Warwickshire
Height: 1.88m (6ft 2in)
Clubs: Stoke City, Man United, Watford (loan), Birmingham City
International:
England

PLAYERS ARE ALWAYS TOLD THERE IS NO LIFE IF YOU LEAVE MANCHESTER UNITED. SHOT-STOPPER BEN FOSTER HAS PROVED THAT WRONG AND EARNED HIMSELF A PLACE IN THE ENGLAND SQUAD.

FOSTER ON...

BEING A KEEPER

"I think playing is a very important part of learning as a goalkeeper. You can only do a certain amount of things on a training field. When you are in front of 70,000 people you find out what you are really capable of. Some fail under that pressure, some thrive on it. I like that sort of pressure."

STOKE SCOUT COLIN DOBSON

"After coming to see me one night, Colin came to watch a few more times. I owe him everything. He is a top man. I don't know what I would have done if Colin hadn't spotted me."

JOINING BIRMINGHAM CITY

"A club like Man United is cut throat, win at all costs, whereas here you know you won't win every game but the players we've got battle and don't give anyone a second breath. At United training is tough and very serious."

7 FOSTER WONDERS

1. Foster hasn't forgotten his culinary skills from when he was a chef and reckons he can knock up anything from a good stew to spaghetti Bolognaise.

2. Although he was at one stage third choice at Man United he was still being picked for the England squad!

3. When he left Man United it was with the blessing of boss Sir Alex Ferguson who said he couldn't stand in the way of the talented shot-stopper.

4. Birmingham paid Man United almost £6m for the keeper – and his team-mates reckon he was worth five times that amount!

5. He always fancied himself as an outfield player but when he was a youngster his two older brothers made him play in goal!

7. Foster scored a penalty in a cup game for Manchester United reserves and says he fancies taking more spot-kicks.

5. Foster was Watford's Player of the Season during his loan at Vicarage Road, during which he helped them to promotion via the play-offs.

FOCUS ON...

BEN FOSTER
The talented keeper who loves pressure

EXTRA TIME: Foster announced that his England career was being put on hold, just before the end of season 2010-11. He'd struggled through the campaign with injury niggles and first wanted to concentrate on getting himself totally fit for club football.

FANTASTIC FOOTIE QUIZ

It's the final round and some of these question are going to be a bit more difficult! We want to know if you are Premier League or non-League!

Answers page 78. No cheating – one point for every correct answer.

1. Spain won the 2010 World Cup – but who were Champions at Germany 2006?

2. Man United, Arsenal, Chelsea – and which other team has won the Premier League?

3. How many times did Thierry Henry win the PFA Player of the Year award? One, two or three?

4. How old was Wayne Rooney when he made his full England debut? 17, 18 or 19?

5. Theo Walcott hadn't scored for England before his hat-trick against Croatia in 2008. True or false?

PART 4: THE FULL GAME

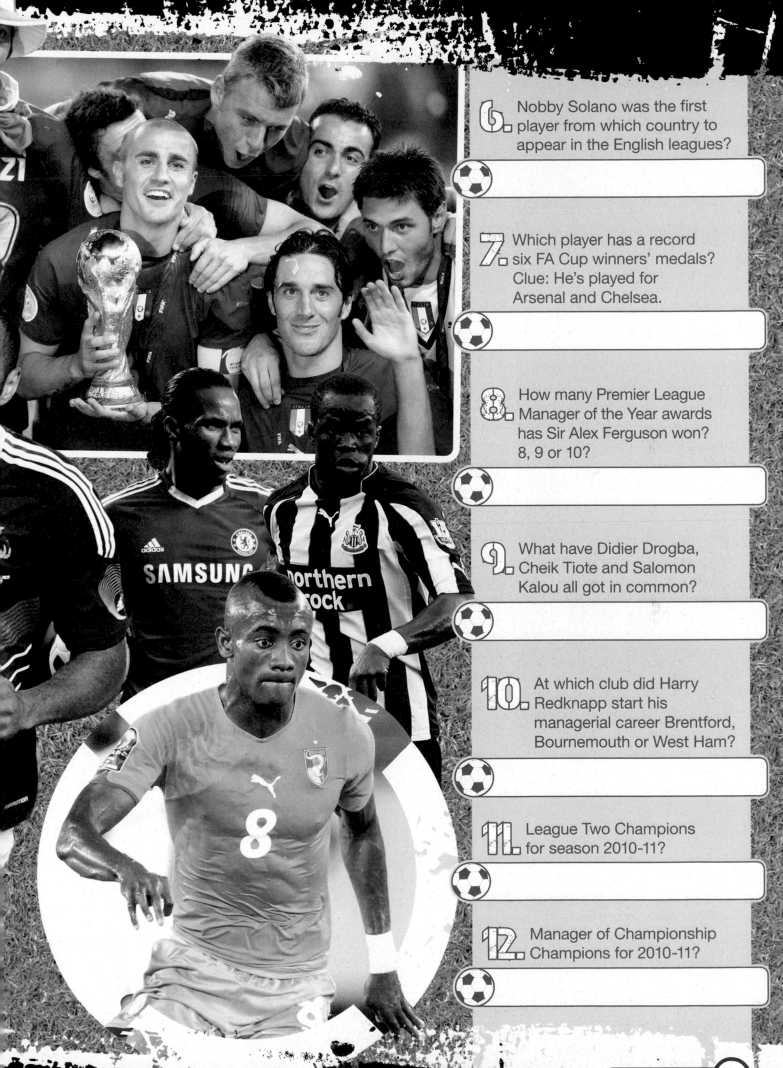

6. Nobby Solano was the first player from which country to appear in the English leagues?

7. Which player has a record six FA Cup winners' medals? Clue: He's played for Arsenal and Chelsea.

8. How many Premier League Manager of the Year awards has Sir Alex Ferguson won? 8, 9 or 10?

9. What have Didier Drogba, Cheik Tiote and Salomon Kalou all got in common?

10. At which club did Harry Redknapp start his managerial career Brentford, Bournemouth or West Ham?

11. League Two Champions for season 2010-11?

12. Manager of Championship Champions for 2010-11?

LEGENDS!

Keepers are often branded as crackers. Here's the proof with some legendary quotes from the past...

That's nuts!
"You shouldn't be nuts but it doesn't matter if you are a bit peculiar."
We won't argue – former Man United star Peter Schmeichel is a very big guy!

Keep on dreaming
"I dreamt of playing for a club like Manchester United and now here I am at Liverpool."
Sander Westerveld proves dreams don't alway come true!

Back to the future
"If you stand still there is only one way to go – and that's backwards."
Not so logicial ex-England keeper Peter Shilton...

Next please!
"It's not nice going to the supermarket and the woman on the till thinking 'dodgy keeper'."
Maybe David – once known as Calamity – James should do his shopping on-line!

THEY SAID WHAT?

We love it when bosses and players launch into full on rants or come out with something totally stupid. Here are a few quotes to get you smiling…

Eyes Down
"We'll show him the sights of Sunderland. We'll take him to the Mecca Bingo to help him settle in."

Sulley Muntari got the guided tour from boss Steve Bruce – who forgot the club's shirt sponsors were also in the full house game!

Goals galore
"We score goals, we let goals in, we score more goals and let more in. We attack, we score goals, we go for it every game."

You don't see many bore draws when Harry Redknapp is in charge of your team!

EXTRA TIME: David James is the oldest keeper to appear in an FA Cup Final. He was less than three months away from his 40th birthday when he turned out for Portsmouth in the 1-0 defeat to Chelsea in 2010

Double top

"I went into the trophy room where they keep all their silverware and I said 'it's lovely, a lot like mine only smaller. They all laughed'."

Port Vale fan and umpteen-times World Darts Champion Phil 'The Power' Taylor couldn't resist a dig on a visit to Old Trafford.

Happy daze

"Avram is not what you think he is. He laughs ever single day with us."

Striker Frédéric Piquionne saw a different West Ham manager to the rest of us...

WHO SAID THAT?

Now it's your turn.
Match the football personalities in the list with the quotes below...

A "I didn't see that particular incident."

B "Please don't call me arrogant, but I'm European champion and I think I'm a special one."

C "You will never get a better chance to win a match than that. My missus could have scored that one."

D "At the end of this game, the European Cup will be only six feet away from you and you'll not even be able to touch it if we lose."

E "...and I'll tell you honestly, I will love it if we beat them – LOVE IT!"

F "When the seagulls follow the trawler, it is because they think sardines will be thrown into the sea".

○ JOSE MOURINHO   ○ KEVIN KEEGAN   ○ HARRY REDKNAPP

○ SIR ALEX FERGUSON   ○ ERIC CANTONA   ○ ARSENE WENGER

EXTRA TIME: Arsene Wenger became manager of Arsenal in 1996 after he left Japan's Grampus Eight, whose playing staff once included BBC TV's Match of the Day presenter Gary Lineker. Wenger was also boss at Nancy-Lorraine and Monaco.

SHOOT ANNUAL 2012 **45**

FOCUS ON...

SERGIO RAMOS
Spain's buccaneering defender

FACT FILE

SERGIO RAMOS GARCIA
Position: Defender
Birth date: March 30, 1986
Birth place: Andalucia, Spain
Height: 1.83m (6ft)
Clubs: Sevilla, Real Madrid
International: Spain

HE'S PICKED UP HIS FAIR SHARE OF RED CARDS BUT SERGIO RAMOS IS STILL ONE OF THE FIRST NAMES ON THE TEAM-SHEET FOR REAL MADRID AND SPAIN. AT THE AGE OF 25 HE'S ALREADY WELL ON HIS WAY TO 80 CAPS FOR HIS COUNTRY AND MADE MORE THAN 300 CLUB APPEARANCES.

RAMOS ON...
REAL MADRID SQUAD'S SUCCESS

"It is important that all men on the squad get playing time. We all have the same excitement and we all want to help out. The squad as a whole is what really matters, not individual players. We are all equally important and we live up to expectations on the pitch."

MADRID'S FANATICAL SUPPORTERS

"It's the fans who have to score the first goal for us. Every visiting side at the Bernabeu has to be wary of the atmosphere. They must really be aware of what it means to play at a stadium like ours. Our fans are essential to us and they are the ones we are really grateful to."

MANAGER JOSE MOURINHO

"He is as relaxed as he always is. The coach never changes his philosophy, style and habits. He has a clear idea of what he wants and we will continue to work in the same way. Mourinho is the captain of our ship and we are with him into death."

THE BOSS'S VIEW
VICENTE DEL BOSQUE SPAIN

"Sergio has the capacity to play anywhere – there are people who believe he could be a good midfielder."

 ## RAMOS WONDERS

1. Ramos' brother Rene was the first member of the family to play football, but now acts as Sergio's agent.

2. The defender joined Real Madrid from Sevilla in 2005 for £23m when he was still just 19.

3. Man United, Chelsea and AC Milan have been linked to moves for the defender.

4. He proudly wears the No.4 shirt, once worn by Fernando Hierro, Madrid's former captain.

5. Ramos can play central defence, right back or even as a defensive midfielder.

6. He was just 18 when he made his debut for Spain and has since won the European Championships and World Cup with his country.

7. Ramos has won a host of individual honours that include being voted into the all-star team at World Cup 2010 and named as UEFA's best defender in 2005-06.

EXTRA TIME: Ramos dropped the Copa del Rey, the Spanish Cup, under the wheels of the team bus in 2011, 18 years after a Real Madrid player last had hands on the trophy. He waved to excited fans from the open top deck during celebrations.

THE BOSS'S VIEW
PEP GUARDIOLA BARCELONA

"I like the love he has for football and his anonymous character. Of course he is one of Barcelona's best-ever players. We just have to enjoy having a player like him in our ranks."

⚽ FACT FILE

LIONEL ANDRES MESSI

Position: Midfielder
Birth date: June 24, 1987
Birth place: Rosario, Argentina
Height: 1.69m (5ft 7in)
Clubs: Barcelona
International: Argentina

TWICE WORLD PLAYER OF THE YEAR AND WITH ENOUGH SILVERWARE TO FILL A WHOLE SERIES OF DISPLAY CABINETS – MESSI REALLY IS A MAGICIAN WITH THE BALL AT HIS FEET.

MESSI ON...

BEING COMPARED TO MARADONA

"I don't want to say that. Even after a million years I will not be as good as him. Maradona was the greatest of all time. I am flattered people even mention me in the same sentence."

BIGGEST DREAM

"I want to write my own history, my own accomplishments. I would swap all my individual prizes to lift the World Cup, that is my biggest dream. Argentina have the best fans in the world when it comes to geeing up the team and psyching us up, there is no other set of fans to match ours."

WAYNE ROONEY

"I have played against him and he doesn't let any occasion get to him. When he is on the pitch it is just him and the ball. Rooney scored a Champions League hat-trick on his debut, that is as much to do with no fear as it is talent."

⑦ MESSI WONDERS

1. Messi started his own foundation that is funded by some of the cash that he earns for promotion and sponsorship work.

2. He says that money doesn't matter to him – that his football is more important, and when he has the ball at his feet he thinks of nothing else.

3. Boss Arsene Wenger called him PlayStation after Messi had smashed four past Arsenal… as he was "out of this world."

4. Modest Messi was in awe after getting the No.10 shirt at Barca as it had previously been worn by his hero Ronaldinho.

5. Messi was European and World Player of the Year in 2009. He won the combined award in 2010.

6. Messi says he will only become a legend if he helps his country with the World Cup.

7. When Messi won the 2009 Ballon d'Or – European Footballer of the Year – he picked up a record 473 points from a possible 480 - a staggering 240 points ahead of his nearest rival, Cristiano Ronaldo.

LIONEL MESSI
Barcelona and Argentina's brilliant forward

FOCUS ON...

EXTRA TIME: After Messi has helped Barcelona beat Manchester United in the 2011 Champions League Final at Wembley he was valued at a staggering £226m! The player has stated that he never wants to leave Barca.

SHOOT ANNUAL 2012 **47**

ALL THE WINNERS

WHO WON WHAT IN 2010-2011

CHAMPIONSHIP CHAMPIONS

QUEEN'S PARK RANGERS

AUTOMATIC PROMOTION	PLAY-OFF FINAL
NORWICH CITY	SWANSEA CITY 4 READING 2

RELEGATED
PRESTON NORTH END, SHEFFIELD UNITED
SCUNTHORPE UNITED

LEAGUE ONE CHAMPIONS

BRIGHTON AND HOVE ALBION

AUTOMATIC PROMOTION	PLAY-OFF FINAL
SOUTHAMPTON	PETERBOROUGH 3 HUDDERSFIELD 0

RELEGATED
DAGENHAM AND REDBRIDGE, BRISTOL ROVERS,
PLYMOUTH ARGYLE, SWINDON TOWN

LEAGUE TWO CHAMPIONS

CHESTERFIELD

AUTOMATIC PROMOTION	PLAY-OFF FINAL
BURY, WYCOMBE	STEVENAGE 1 TORQUAY 0

RELEGATED
LINCOLN CITY, STOCKPORT COUNTY

BLUE SQUARE CHAMPIONS

CRAWLEY TOWN

PLAY-OFF FINAL
AFC WIMBLEDON 0   LUTON TOWN 0
AFC WIMBLEDON WON 4-3 ON PENS

EXTRA TIME: AFC Wimbledon, created when the original Wimbledon side changed its name to MK Dons and moved to Milton Keynes in 2002, were promoted six times before finally earning their place in League Two for season 2011-12.

SCOTTISH PREMIER LEAGUE

RANGERS

Boss Walter Smith bowed out with his third title in a row, his tenth in all with the Ibrox club, with a final day of the season 5-1 hammering of Kilmarnock. Gers had just one point to spare over bitter rivals Celtic.

SCOTTISH CUP

CELTIC

The Bhoys stopped Rangers' clean sweep of silverware in Scotland by winning 3-0 against Motherwell. It was boss Neil Lennon's first trophy for the club with goals from Ki Sung-Yong, Craigan and Mulgrew.

CIS CUP

RANGERS

The blue half of the Old Firm were celebrating after a 2-1 victory over Celtic. Rangers took the lead after 31 through Steven Davis, Joe Ledley equalised for the Bhoys before Nikica Jelavic's winner eight minutes into extra time.

LEAGUE CUP

BIRMINGHAM CITY

Blues' skipper Stephen Carr had hung up his boots in May 2008 – but was persuaded out of retirement and helped guide City to their first major trophy since 1963. Nikola Zigic gave Birmingham the lead, Robin van Persie equalised, and then late substitute Obafemi Martins scored the winner in the last minute.

FA CUP

MANCHESTER CITY

Having qualified for their first crack at the Champions League just a week earlier, City added their first trophy in 35 years when they beat Stoke 1-0 at Wembley. Yaya Toure was the man who earned their final appearances with his semi-final strike against Manchester United – and City lifted the cup thanks to his 74th minute winner in the final.

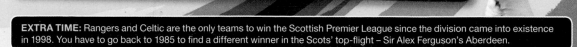

EXTRA TIME: Rangers and Celtic are the only teams to win the Scottish Premier League since the division came into existence in 1998. You have to go back to 1985 to find a different winner in the Scots' top-flight – Sir Alex Ferguson's Aberdeen.

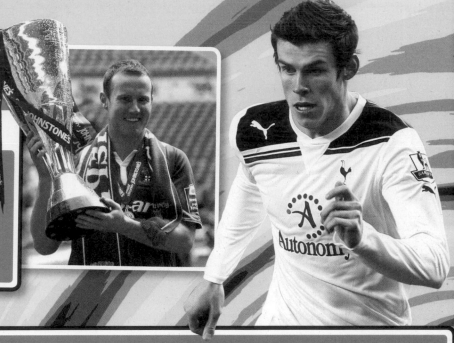

JOHNSTONE'S PAINTS TROPHY

CARLISLE

Carlisle returned to Wembley for their second JPT Final in two years – but this time went home with the silverware thanks to their 1-0 win over Brentford. The previous season they were beaten 4-1 by Southampton. This time Peter Murphy gave them victory in the 12th minute.

PFA AND FOOTBALL WRITERS' PLAYERS OF THE YEAR

GARETH BALE & SCOTT PARKER

Gareth Bale's stunning form at the start of the season meant he had the PFA award sewn up before Christmas! The Wales defender-winger added millions to his value with some stunning displays, raiding down the left and topped off with a hat-trick against AC Milan. Scott Parker suffered relegation with West Ham – but won the Football Writers' Award. The midfielder was a bright light in a gloomy season for the Hammers and earned himself an England recall.

PFA YOUNG PLAYER OF THE YEAR

JACK WILSHERE

There was no surprise that Jack Wilshere won this award having played like a veteran for Arsenal before pulling on an England shirt and looking so at home in midfield. Just 19, he finished ahead of Gareth Bale, who had won the senior award, and Man United striker Javier Hernandez.

THE FA TROPHY FINAL
DARLINGTON 1
MANSFIELD 0

Chris Senior scored the only goal at Wembley in the final minute of extra-time with 10,000 Quakers fans in the crowd of 25,000.

THE FA VASE
COALVILLE TOWN 2
WHITLEY BAY 3

Bay lifted their third Vase in three years, their fourth in total. Paul Chow, who had scored in the Seahorses' last two final victories, added two more to his Wembley tally.

EUROPA LEAGUE FINAL
PORTO 1
BRAGA 0

Colombian striker Falcao scored with a diving header just before half-time to seal victory. It was his 17th goal in the competition.

SPAIN	ITALY	FRANCE	GERMANY	HOLLAND
CHAMPIONS	**CHAMPIONS**	**CHAMPIONS**	**CHAMPIONS**	**CHAMPIONS**
BARCELONA	AC MILAN	LILLE	BORUSSIA DORTMUND	AJAX
RUNNERS-UP	**RUNNERS-UP**	**RUNNERS-UP**	**RUNNERS-UP**	**RUNNERS-UP**
REAL MADRID	INTER MILAN	MARSEILLE	BAYER LEVERKUSEN	FC TWENTE

EXTRA TIME: The PFA Player of the Year award has been handed out since 1974 and in that time only four players have won the trophy twice – Mark Hughes, Alan Shearer, Thierry Henry and Cristiano Ronaldo.

YOUR GUIDE TO THE CLUBS

YOUR GUIDE TO THE 20 ENGLISH PREMIER LEAGUES SIDES:
PLUS STAR MEN, LEGENDS, STATS, FACTS AND DETAILS FROM SEASON 2010-11

ARSENAL

FOUNDED: 1886
GROUND: EMIRATES STADIUM
CAPACITY: 60,355
NICKNAME: GUNNERS

HONOURS
League Champions: 1931, 1933, 1934, 1935, 1938, 1948, 1953, 1971, 1989, 1991, 1998, 2002, 2004
FA Cup: 1930, 1936, 1950, 1971, 1979, 1993, 1998, 2002, 2003, 2005
League Cup: 1987, 1993
European Fairs Cup: 1970
European Cup Winners' Cup: 1994

PREMIER LEAGUE
Time in Prem: 1992-present
Best finish: Champions (1998, 2002, 2004)

SEASON 2010-11
Position: 4th
Top scorer: Robin van Persie, 21
Player of the Season: Jack Wilshere

LEGEND
Thierry Henry 1999-07
A winger when he arrived at Highbury, the France star was converted to a striker by Arsene Wenger and had a devastating impact on the team. Speed, finishing, skills… Henry had the lot and 380 appearances later he had hit a record 226 goals for the club, a record that still stands. Bought for £10m from Juventus and sold for £16m to Barcelona, he is still idolised by Gunners fans.

STAR PLAYER
Robin van Persie 2004-present
The Holland forward was just 20 when he arrived at Arsenal from Feyenoord for just £2.75m. Last campaign was certainly his best for the club in terms of goal-scoring and included his first hat-trick for the Gunners. Injuries have meant that he has missed a lot of football, yet he has still proved a major asset to the side. Boss Arsene Wenger rates him as a very important player.

REMEMBER THIS? Between May 2003 and October 2004 Arsenal went an incredible 49 games unbeaten. They won 36 and drew 13 of their games, picking up the Premier League title along the way. They were dubbed the Invincibles. The run started with an incredible 6-0 win over Southampton and ended in a 2-0 defeat to Manchester United at Old Trafford. What made the run even more satisfying was that Arsenal still stuck to their entertaining brand of football under Arsene Wenger.

LEGEND
Peter Withe 1980-85
The Liverpool-born striker played for a whole host of clubs but it was at Villa where he most made his mark, helping them to both the English League title and the European Cup. The outlay of £500,000 to Newcastle on a player who was then 29 and regarded as nothing more than a decent striker proved to be cash very well spent!

STAR PLAYER
Darren Bent 2011-present
When Villa forked out a club record fee to take Bent from Sunderland in the January 2011 transfer window many fans thought they had paid too much. But the former Tottenham, Charton and Ipswich striker helped spark a Villans revival by scoring the goals that pushed them away from relegation. He cost an initial £18m but the figure is likely to rise to £24m – double what Sunderland paid to Spurs for the player.

ASTON VILLA

FOUNDED: 1974
GROUND: VILLA PARK
CAPACITY: 42,786
NICKNAME: VILLANS

HONOURS
League Champions: 1894, 1896, 1897, 1899, 1900, 1910, 1981
FA Cup: 1887, 1895, 1897, 1905, 1913, 1920, 1957
League Cup: 1961, 1975, 1977, 1994, 1996
European Cup: 1982
European Super Cup: 1983

PREMIER LEAGUE
Time in Prem: 1992-present
Best finish: Runners-up (1993)

SEASON 2010-11
Position: 9th
Top scorer: Stewart Downing, Darren Bent, Ashley Young, 7
Player of the Season: Stewart Downing

REMEMBER THIS?
Peter Withe and Gary Shaw both scored three goals as the Villans marched to European Cup glory under boss Tony Barton. Withe not only scored the solitary goal of the final as German giants Bayern Munich were put to the sword, he was also voted Man of the Match.

BLACKBURN ROVERS

HONOURS
League Champions: 1912, 1914, 1995
Division Two: 1939
Division Two play-off winners 1992
Division Three: 1975
FA Cup:
1884, 1885, 1886, 1890, 1891, 1928
League Cup: 2002
Full Members Cup: 1987

PREMIER LEAGUE
Time in Prem: 1992-99, 01-present
Best finish: Champions (1995)

SEASON 2010-11
Position: 15
Top scorer:
Junior Hoilett, Nikola Kalinic, 6
Player of the Season: Paul Robinson

LEGEND
Simon Garner 1978-92
The striker played 484 league games for Rovers scoring a club record 194 goals. His final season at Ewood Park saw him score goals that helped Blackburn gain promotion and be one of the founder members of the Premier League. He started his career with Rovers when he signed professional in 1978 and left in 1992, before the new league kicked-off, to join West Brom.

STAR PLAYER
Steven N'Zonzi 2009-present
The defensive midfielder cost just £500,000 from Amiens but his first season at Ewood Park was such a success that Rovers soon lengthened his contract to 2015 to ward off would-be approaches. The France Under-21 star, who won the club's Player of the Year award in his first season, was yet another bargain buy picked up by former boss Sam Allardyce.

REMEMBER THIS?
Under boss Kenny Dalglish and with star striker Alan Shearer, Rovers won the Premier League in 1995. They were funded by the millions of then chairman Jack Walker. Four years later Blackburn created history by being the first side to have won the Premier League and be relegated.

LEGEND
John McGinlay 1992-97
The Scotland striker was part of the side that first went up to the Premier League but injuries curtailed his appearances. He also helped shoot them back to the top-flight, contributing 24 to their 100-goal tally in the second tier. It included the last goal scored at former ground Burnden Park.

BOLTON WANDERERS

STAR PLAYER
Kevin Davies 2003-present
The inspirational Reebok skipper isn't the most prolific marksman but his all-round forward play makes him a valuable asset to the side. Well capable of playing as a sole frontman, Davies is strong enough to win aerial challenges and is often asked to hold up the ball to allow his team-mates to burst forwards. He played for Chesterfield, Blackburn and Southampton before joining Bolton on a free. Davies' won the club's Player of the Year award in his first season.

HONOURS
First division: 1997
Second division: 1909, 1978
Third division: 1973
Division One play-off winners: 1995, 2001
FA Cup: 1923, 1926, 1929, 1958
Football League Trophy: 1989

PREMIER LEAGUE
Time in Prem: 1995-96, 97-98, 01-present
Best finish: 6th (2005)

SEASON 2010-11
Position: 14th
Top scorer: Johan Elmander, 12
Player of the Season: Stuart Holden

REMEMBER THIS? The 4-3 play-off victory over Reading in 1995 that ended Bolton's 15-year exile from the top-flight. Wanderers had been 2-0 down at half-time but manager Bruce Rioch gave them a rousing speech. Their arrival in the Premier League came after a spell that had seen the team plunge to the league's basement division.

CHELSEA

LEGEND
Gianfranco Zola
1996-03
The diminutive striker played with skill, style and a smile and it was no surprise when fans voted him the Blues' best-ever player. Two FA Cups, a League Cup, Cup Winners' Cup and UEFA Super Cup were highlights of his career at the Bridge – and all before Abramovich's cash brought in big-money buys.

STAR PLAYER
Frank Lampard 2001-present
The midfielder's £11m move across London from West Ham raised a few eyebrows. Many fans thought boss Claudio Ranieri had paid over the odds. How wrong they were! Lamps was named the Premier League Player of the Decade in 2009, has scored more goals than any other Chelsea midfielder ever, is the highest midfield scorer in Premier League history and made more than 500 appearances in a Blues shirt.

FOUNDED: 1905
GROUND: STAMFORD BRIDGE
CAPACITY: 41,841
NICKNAME: BLUES/PENSIONERS

HONOURS
League Champions:
1955, 2005, 2006, 2010
Division Two: 1984, 1989
FA Cup: 1970, 1997, 2000, 2007, 2009, 2010
League Cup: 1965, 1998, 2005, 2007
Cup Winners Cup: 1971, 1998
UEFA Super Cup: 1998

PREMIER LEAGUE
Time in Prem: 1992-present
Best finish: Champions (2005, 2006, 2010)

SEASON 2010-11
Position: 2nd
Top scorer: Nicolas Anelka, 16
Player of the Season: Petr Cech

REMEMBER THIS?
The arrival of Jose Mourinho in 2004 and Chelsea going on to win back-to-back titles in 2005 and 2006. The first was their first title in 50 years and the second made them only the fifth side since the Second World War to win the title twice in a row. They won their third Premier League title under Carlo Ancelotti.

LEGEND
Duncan Ferguson 1994-98, 00-06
Set a British record when he moved from Rangers for £4m in 1994 after a loan spell to start his love affair with the Toffees. An FA Cup-winner with Everton, Scotland star Big Dunc was a feared no-nonsense striker, praised for his heading ability but no slouch when it came to footwork either. Sold to Newcastle but then bought back.

STAR PLAYER
Tim Cahill 2004-present
At just £1.5m from Millwall, Cahill has to be one of the best-ever buys ever made by Everton. His drive, determination, will to win and goals have made him a vital asset to the Goodison Park team. A glut of goals in the Merseyside derby hasn't done his status any harm amongst Evertonians! The Australia star scores with both feet and has one of the best records in the top-flight for headed goals.

EVERTON

FOUNDED: 1878
GROUND: GOODISON PARK
CAPACITY: 40,157
NICKNAME: TOFFEES

HONOURS
League Champions: 1891, 1915, 1928, 1932, 1939, 1963, 1970, 1985, 1987
Division Two: 1931
FA Cup: 1906 1933, 1966, 1984, 1995
European Cup Winners Cup: 1985

PREMIER LEAGUE
Time in Prem: 1992-present
Best finish: 4th (2005)

SEASON 2010-11
Position: 7th
Top scorer: Louis Saha, 10
Player of the Season: Leighton Baines

REMEMBER THIS? The 1984-85 season ended with Everton lifting English football's top-flight title with four games to spare! They also won the Cup Winners' Cup but lost out in the FA Cup Final to Manchester United. Due to English clubs being banned from Europe at that time, the Toffees missed out on a crack at the European Cup.

FULHAM

FOUNDED: 1879
GROUND: CRAVEN COTTAGE
CAPACITY: 25,700
NICKNAME: COTTAGERS

HONOURS
Division One: 2001
Division Two: 1949, 1999
Division Three (South): 1932

PREMIER LEAGUE
Time in Prem: 2001-present
Best finish: 7th (2009)

SEASON 2010-11
Position: 8th
Top scorer: Clint Dempsey, 12
Player of the Season:
Clint Dempsey

LEGEND
Gordon Davies
1978-84, 86-91
The Wales striker hit 178 goals in 450 appearances for the Cottagers to etch his place in West London folklore – not least because he hit a hat-trick against rivals Chelsea. He played for Chelsea and Manchester City between his two spells at Craven Cottage.

STAR PLAYER
Bobby Zamora 2008-present
Fulham fans have probably seen the best of the much-travelled striker in the top-flight. Always a skilled player, Bobby Z hasn't always been able to turn his promise and commitment into goals. He's improved all round at Craven Cottage, so much so that he pushed his way into the England squad. Zamora arrived at Fulham from West Ham for around £5m having played for Bristol Rovers, Brighton and Tottenham.

REMEMBER THIS? Fulham lost the 2010 Europa League Final 2-1 against Atletico Madrid after extra time but there are few fans who will ever forget their amazing journey to Germany for that match! On their way to the final Fulham had dismissed Shakhtar Donetsk, Juventus, Wolfsburg and Hamburg. They'd needed four goals against Juve and won the home leg 4-1, the tie on aggregate 5-4!

LEGEND
Kenny Dalglish 1977-90
Dalglish's place in Reds' history is cemented thanks to his time as both a player and manager with the club. He turned out a total of 501 times for Liverpool between 1977 and 1990 after arriving from Celtic, showing the creativity and finishing that left fans sitting on the edges of their seats. As boss in his first spell at Anfield he won the Division One title in 1986, 1988 and 1990.

LIVERPOOL

FOUNDED: 1892 **GROUND:** ANFIELD
CAPACITY: 42,276 **NICKNAME:** REDS

HONOURS
League Champions:
1901, 1906, 1922, 1923, 1947, 1964, 1966, 1973, 1976, 1977, 1979, 1980, 1982, 1983, 1984, 1986, 1988, 1990
FA Cup: 1965, 1974, 1986, 1989, 1992, 2001, 2006
League Cup: 1981, 1982, 1983, 1984, 1995, 2001, 2003
European Cup:
1977, 1978, 1981, 1984, 2005
UEFA Cup: 1973, 1976, 2001
European Super Cup: 1977, 2001, 2005
Super Cup: 1986
Division Two: 1894, 1896, 1905, 1962

PREMIER LEAGUE
Time in Prem: 1992-present
Best finish: 2nd (2009)

SEASON 2010-11
Position: 6th
Top scorer: Dirk Kuyt, 13
Player of the Season:
Lucas Leiva

STAR PLAYER
Steven Gerrard 1998-present
Wide or central midfield, Gerrard will always influence a game and put in a shift for the side he supported from the Kop as a boy. Stevie G is a one-club player who rejected Chelsea's advances and has now passed the 500 games mark for the Reds, hitting more than 130 goals in the process.

REMEMBER THIS? Dead at 3-0 down to AC Milan at half-time in the 2005 Champions League Final in Istanbul, Liverpool refused to be buried. Gerrard inspired their comeback nine minutes after the break, Vladimir Smicer made it 3-2 and on the hour mark Xabi Alonso's equaliser ensured extra-time. Jerzy Dudek's penalty save from Andriy Shevchenko gave Liverpool victory in the shoot-out.

MANCHESTER CITY

FOUNDED: 1880
GROUND: CITY OF MANCHESTER STADIUM (EASTLANDS)
CAPACITY: 47,700
NICKNAME: CITIZENS, BLUES

HONOURS
League Champions: 1937, 1968
Division One: 2002
Division Two play-off winners: 1999
Division Two: 1899, 1903, 1910, 1928, 1947, 1966
FA Cup: 1904, 1934, 1956, 1969
League Cup: 1970, 1976
European Cup Winners' Cup: 1970

PREMIER LEAGUE
Time in Prem:
92-96, 00-01, 02-present
Best finish: 3rd (2011)

SEASON 2010-11
Position: 3rd
Top scorer: Carlos Tevez, 21
Player of the Season:
Vincent Kompany

STAR PLAYER:
David Silva 2010-present
The Spain midfielder arrived at Eastlands in summer 2010 for £24m from Valencia. Despite a slow start he has now proved to be one of City's key creative and exciting players. Three Player of the Month awards before the start of 2011 showed what a great signing he was! Many fans saw him as their Player of the Season. Still only 25, he already has European Championship and World Cup winners' medals. Made his Spain debut at the age of 20.

REMEMBER THIS? City were relegated from the Premier League in 1996, dropped a further division in 1998, and arrived back in the Premier League in 2000 for just one season. They got back into the top-flight under Kevin Keegan in 2002. In 2008, a big-money Mid-East takeover launched their bid to become one of the biggest teams in the world.

LEGEND
Eric Cantona 1992-97
One of Sir Alex Ferguson's most important signings ever. Plucked from rivals Leeds United for just £1.2m, the France forward proved to be the catalyst to help United start on their incredible silverware trail, starting with the first-ever Premier League in 1992-93. Cantona would pick up three more titles during his time at Old Trafford, despite a lengthy ban for a kung-fu style kick on a Crystal Palace fan.

MANCHESTER UNITED

FOUNDED: 1878
GROUND: OLD TRAFFORD
CAPACITY: 75,957
NICKNAME: RED DEVILS

HONOURS
League Champions: 1908, 1911, 1952, 1956, 1957, 1965, 1967, 1993, 1994, 1996, 1997, 1999, 2000, 2001, 2003, 2007, 2008, 2009, 2011
Division Two: 1936, 1975
FA Cup: 1909, 1948, 1963, 1977, 1983, 1985, 1990, 1994, 1996, 1999, 2004
League Cup: 1992, 2006, 2009, 2010
European Cup: 1968, 1999, 2008
UEFA Cup Winners Cup: 1991
UEFA Super Cup: 1991
Intercontinental Cup: 1999
FIFA Club World Cup: 2008

PREMIER LEAGUE
Time in Prem: 1992-present
Best finish: Champions (12 times)

SEASON 2010-11
Position: Champions
Top scorer: Dimitar Berbatov, 21
Player of the Season:
Nemanja Vidic

STAR PLAYER
Wayne Rooney 2004-present
The striker cost £25m from Everton when he was still just 18. The Scouser has had his fair share of off-field problems and temper tantrums, but on the field he has blossomed into one of the best players around. Although he's regarded as a striker, Rooney can also play in midfield and just behind the frontman to devastating effect.

REMEMBER THIS? The year was 1999 and United scored a unique Treble of Premier League, FA Cup and European Cup. But most remarkable was their victory in Europe where the Red Devils bounced back from a goal down to win in time added on, thanks to goals from Teddy Sheringham and Ole Gunnar Solskjaer.

NEWCASTLE UNITED

FOUNDED: 1892
GROUND: ST. JAMES' PARK
CAPACITY: 52,380
NICKNAME: MAGPIES/TOON

HONOURS
League Champions:
1905, 1907, 1909, 1927
Championship: 2010
First Division: 1993
Second Division: 1965
FA Cup: 1910, 1924, 1932, 1951, 1952, 1955
Inter Cities Fairs Cup: 1969

PREMIER LEAGUE
Time in Prem: 1994-09, 2010-present
Best finish: 2nd (1996, 1997)

SEASON 2010-11
Position: 12th
Top scorer: Kevin Nolan, 12
Player of the Season: Joey Barton

LEGEND
Alan Shearer 1996-06
Ten years with his home town club after a then record £15m move from Blackburn Rovers turned him into a Tyneside mega-hero. The sparkling new bar under the Gallowgate stand, where he used to watch matches as a kid, is named Shearer's. His 206 goals for the Toon is a record – as are the 260 Premier League goals the former England captain scored during his career.

STAR PLAYER
Steven Taylor 2003-present
Made his debut in 2004 thanks to Bobby Robson. Despite constant speculation linking him with moves away from the Toon, the central defender always wanted to stay put. Supported Newcastle as a boy, grew up a black and white and committed himself to United to 2016 – effectively making him a one-club player if he sees out the deal. The No.27 is worn in honour of previous holders Philippe Albert and Jonathan Woodgate.

REMEMBER THIS? Sir Bobby Robson got a hero's welcome when he took over as boss of the club he had supported as a boy growing up in County Durham. His first home game resulted in a staggering 8-0 victory over Sheffield Wednesday in September 1999. It was the club's first home win since February and Alan Shearer hit five of the goals.

LEGEND
Bryan Gunn 1986-98
The Scotland keeper played 478 games for the Canaries after joining from Aberdeen. City's shock victory at Bayern Munich in the 1993-94 UEFA Cup second round is often credited to the amazing saves he pulled off during the 2-1 win. Twice voted Norwich's Player of the Year before departing for Hibs. Later had a short, difficult spell as Carrow Road manager.

STAR PLAYER
Grant Holt 2009-present
From non-league through to the Premier League, Holt finally earned his right to play in the top-flight at the age of 30. The striker has been the club's Player of the Season for the past two years with a total of 53 goals in those campaigns. The former Sheffield Wednesday, Rochdale and Nottingham Forest frontman arrived from Shrewsbury for just under £500,000.

NORWICH CITY

FOUNDED: 1902
GROUND: CARROW ROAD
CAPACITY: 27,000
NICKNAME: CANARIES, YELLOWS

HONOURS
League One: 2010
First Division: 2004
Division Two: 1972, 1986
Division Three: 1933
League Cup: 1962, 1985

PREMIER LEAGUE
Time in Prem:
1992-95, 04-05, 2011-
Best finish: 3rd (1993)

SEASON 2010-11
Position: Championship runners-up
Top scorer: Grant Holt, 23
Player of the Season: Grant Holt

REMEMBER THIS? Norwich finished third in the first-ever Premier League in 1992-93 but in 1995 they were relegated. At the end of 2003-04 they returned to the top-flight for one season. They spent three seasons in the Championship before dropping to the third tier of English football for one season, winning League One in 2010 and returning to the Premier League in 2011.

QUEENS PARK RANGERS

FOUNDED: 1882
GROUND: LOFTUS ROAD
CAPACITY: 19,100
NICKNAME: HOOPS, RANGERS, RS

HONOURS
Championship: 2011
Division Two: 1983
Division Three: 1967
League Cup: 1967

PREMIER LEAGUE
Time in Prem: 1992-96, 2011-
Best finish: 5th (1993)

SEASON 2010-11
Position: Championship champions
Top scorer: Adel Taarabt, 19
Player of the Season: Paddy Kenny

LEGEND
Les Ferdinand 1987-1995
Sold to Newcastle for a QPR record of £6m, losing the England striker was a massive blow at Loftus Road and many believed it contributed to the club's relegation the following season. Sir Les had arrived from non-league Hayes and went on to score 80 goals in 163 league games.

STAR PLAYER
Adel Taarabt 2010-present
The Moroccan midfielder was deemed surplus to requirements at Tottenham and QPR, where he had enjoyed successful loans, stepped in. He was 2010-11 Championship Player of the Year, and showed the kind of skill that R's fans just love to see. His dribbling, passing, trickery and goal-scoring were all impressive and there were reports he had been watched by Manchester United.

REMEMBER THIS? It was season 1987-88 and under manager, Jim Smith, Rangers finished fifth in the top-flight to become London's leading side that campaign. They were a point above Arsenal and local rivals Chelsea were relegated. Since then they have dropped as low as the third tier of English football and had to battle against major financial problems.

LEGEND
Sir Stanley Matthews
1932-47, 61-65
The oldest player to turn out in England's top-flight, and for his country, Sir Stanley was still playing at the age of 70! One of the first players in the English Football Hall of Fame, the former European Player of the Year made 794 career appearances and scored 82 goals. The locally born winger made a total of 352 appearances for the Potters and is thought to have played more than 2,000 games before quitting totally.

STAR PLAYER
Matthew Etherington 2009-present
Arguably playing some of the best football of a career that has taken in Peterborough, Tottenham and West Ham. The left winger never really got a chance at Spurs, was a hit with the Hammers but has excelled at Stoke City after a £2m move. Pace and the ability to drift past defenders has made him a firm fans' favourite at the Britannia Stadium.

STOKE CITY

FOUNDED: 1863
GROUND: BRITANNIA STADIUM
CAPACITY: 28,383
NICKNAME: POTTERS

HONOURS
Division Two: 1933, 1963, 1993
Division Two play-off winners: 2002
Division Three (North): 1927
League Cup: 1972
Auto Windscreen Shield: 2000
Autoglass Trophy: 1992

PREMIER LEAGUE
Time in Prem: 2008-present
Best finish: 11th (2010)

SEASON 2010-11
Position: 13th
Top scorer: Jon Walters, Kenwyne Jones, both 12
Player of the Season: Robert Huth

REMEMBER THIS? The 2011 FA Cup defeat to Manchester City is still a day to be remembered as it was the Potters' first appearance in the final in their 148-year history. Despite defeat, it meant that Stoke qualified for European competition for only the third time ever and the first occasion in almost 40 years.

SUNDERLAND

FOUNDED: 1879
GROUND: STADIUM OF LIGHT
CAPACITY: 49,000
NICKNAME: BLACK CATS

HONOURS
League Champions:
1892, 1893, 1895, 1902, 1913, 1936
Championship: 2005, 2007
Division One: 1996, 1999
Second division: 1976
Third division: 1988
FA Cup: 1937, 1973

PREMIER LEAGUE
Time in Prem: 1996-97, 99-03,
05-06, 07-present
Best finish: 7th (1999, 2000)

SEASON 2010-11
Position: 10th
Top scorer: Asamoah Gyan, 10
Player of the Season: Phil Bardsley

LEGEND
Kevin Phillips 1997-03
It's no surprise the Wearsiders' fans nicknamed him Super Kev – he cost just £600,000 from Watford and scored an average of almost a goal every other game! The striker played 239 games and hit 134 goals for the Black Cats to become their post-War record goal scorer. Sold to Southampton for £3.25m following Sunderland's relegation in 2003

STAR PLAYER
Lee Cattermole 2009-present
Manager Steve Bruce bought Cattermole from his previous club Wigan for £6m, having taken him to Athletic from Middlesbrough for £3.5m. Combative and hard tackling, the north east-born player is sorely missed when he is either suspended or injured. His disciplinary record has cost him vital time on the pitch but his match-winning abilities did earn him the captaincy.

REMEMBER THIS? The 1973 FA Cup Final goes down in history as a major shock with Sunderland defeating the then mighty Leeds United 1-0 thanks to a super goal from Ian Porterfield. But the game will also be remembered for manager Bob Stoke dancing on the pitch and an incredible double save from keeper Jim Montgomery.

LEGEND
Leon Britton
2002-03, 03-10, 11-
During three spells with Swansea, one on loan, midfielder Britton has clocked up more than 300 appearances for the Swans. He was a player who helped them stay in the Football League and played his part as they won the Championship play-off final at Wembley. The former West Ham trainee had a short spell with Sheffield United in 2010-11, playing 26 games.

SWANSEA CITY

STAR PLAYER
Scott Sinclair 2010-present
His second career hat-trick, scored in the play-off final victory over Reading, means that Sinclair will forever be etched into the history of the Swans. His goals ensured Swansea's return to the top-flight for the first time since 1983 and the appearance of a Welsh side in the Premier League for the first time ever.

FOUNDED: 1912
GROUND: LIBERTY STADIUM
CAPACITY: 20,530
NICKNAME: SWANS, JACKS

HONOURS
Championship:
Play-off winners 2011
League One: 2008
Third Division: 2000
Football League Trophy:
1994, 2006
Welsh Cup:
1913, 1932, 1950, 1961, 1966,
1981, 1982, 1983, 1989, 1991

PREMIER LEAGUE
Time in Prem: 2011-
Best finish: 6th (old Division One)

SEASON 2010-11
Position: 3rd Championship
Top scorer: Scott Sinclair, 27
Player of the Season: Nathan Dyer

REMEMBER THIS? Three promotions in four seasons between 1978 and 1981 saw Swansea rise from the fourth tier of English football to the top-flight. By 1986 they had plunged back to the old Division Four (League Two). Despite financial worries that almost saw the Swans go out of business, they have battled back and built an impressive new ground.

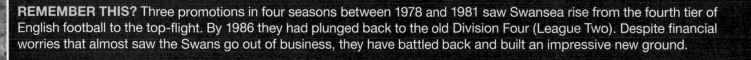

TOTTENHAM HOTSPUR

FOUNDED: 1882
GROUND: WHITE HART LANE
CAPACITY: 36,300
NICKNAME: SPURS

HONOURS
League Champions: 1951, 1961
Division Two: 1920, 1950
FA Cup: 1901, 1921, 1961, 1962, 1967, 1981, 1982, 1991
League Cup: 1971, 1973, 1999, 2008
UEFA Cup: 1972, 1984
UEFA Cup Winners Cup: 1963

PREMIER LEAGUE
Time in Prem: 1992-present
Best finish: 4th (2010)

SEASON 2010-11
Position: 5th
Top scorer: Rafael van der Vaart, 14
Player of the Season: Luka Modric

LEGEND
Teddy Sheringham
1992-97, 01-03
The England striker scored 124 goals in 277 games for Spurs during two spells at White Hart Lane, punctuated by his time with Manchester United. His intelligent play, fantastic link up skills between midfield and the front, plus his all around ability marked him down as the type of player Tottenham fans love.

STAR PLAYER
Aaron Lennon 2005-present
The lightning fast England winger is a player who can turn a game with a burst of speed or a jink past a defender. His pinpoint crosses can provide deadly ammunition for the strikers. Once the Premier League's youngster-ever player, when he turned out for Leeds at the age of 16, he's been hit by injuries but was still selected for his country at the last two World Cup finals.

REMEMBER THIS? Tottenham were 4-0 down with just 35 minutes of the Champions League game gone against Inter Milan. But Gareth Bale wasn't going to settle for that scoreline and hit a brilliant second-half hat-trick, two in the final minutes. That left the first tie at 4-3 at the San Siro – but those goals were vital. Spurs won the second-leg 3-1, inspired again by Bale, as they marched into the last 16 of Europe's top club competition for the first time ever.

LEGEND
Tony Brown 1963-80, 81
Having played a record 720 games and scored a club best of 279 goals for Albion, it's no surprise that Tony Brown will never be forgotten at the Hawthorns! One England cap, three times Midlands Footballer of the Year, an FA Cup and League Cup also gained him entry to the Professional Footballers' Association Hall of Fame.

WEST BROMWICH ALBION

FOUNDED: 1878
GROUND: HAWTHORNS
CAPACITY: 26,500
NICKNAME: BAGGIES

HONOURS
League Champions: 1920
Championship: 2008
Division Two: 1902, 1911
Division Two play-off winners: 1993
FA Cup: 1888, 1892, 1931, 1954, 1968
League Cup: 1966

PREMIER LEAGUE
Time in Prem: 2002-03, 04-06, 08-09, 10-present
Best finish: 11th (2011)

SEASON 2010-11
Position: 11th
Top scorer: Peter Odemwingie, 15
Player of the Season: Youssouf Mulumbu

STAR PLAYER
Youssouf Mulumbu
2009-present
Consistent and combative the Congo midfielder has proved a valuable addition since arriving from Paris Saint Germain. Fans love his effort and at £175,000 he has to be one of the Baggies' best buys ever! A regular Man of the Match winner, as voted by fans at games. Scoring the winner against Villa did him no harm!

REMEMBER THIS? The club that was rock bottom of the Premier League at Christmas always went down – until West Brom defied the history books! Having just returned to the top-flight that season, former player Bryan Robson, who was now managing the side, maintained their status in the top tier on the final day of the 2004-05 season.

WIGAN ATHLETIC

FOUNDED: 1932
GROUND: DW STADIUM
CAPACITY: 25,168
NICKNAME: LATICS

HONOURS
Division Two Champions: 2003
Division Three Champions: 1997
League Trophy: 1985, 1999

PREMIER LEAGUE
Time in Prem: 2005-present
Best finish: 10th (2006)

SEASON 2010-11
Position: 16th
Top scorer:
Charles N'Zogbia, 10
Player of the Season:
Ali al-Habsi

LEGEND
Arjan de Zeeuw
1999-02, 05-07
The Dutch defender spent time with Wigan in Division Two, making more than 130 appearances for them before a move to Portsmouth, where he played in the top-flight. When Wigan reached the Premier League he returned and impressed again before injury cut short his career.

STAR PLAYER
Maynor Figueroa 2008-present
Bought by the club before the departure of boss Steve Bruce, the defender has many admirers and has been linked with moves to bigger sides. Left-footed with brilliant dead-ball skills, the Honduran also has a long throw. On his way to 80 caps for his country, the left back or central defender has now also past the 100-plus league game mark for Athletic. Figueroa had only played in his home country before joining Wigan.

REMEMBER THIS?
Boss Paul Jewell managed them from England's third tier to the top-flight, their automatic promotion to the Premier League confirmed on the final day of the 2003-04 season. A remarkable record for a team that only entered the League in 1978. The manager quit despite ensuring the club's survival against relegation during their second year in the division.

LEGEND
Steve Bull 1986-99
The club's record goalscorer arrived from West Brom and notched an incredible 18 hat-tricks during his time at Molineux, where one of the stands is named after him. Capped 13 times by England, he scored four goals for the international side. Bull can still be spotted supporting Wolves.

STAR PLAYER
Matt Jarvis 2007-present
The former Gillingham winger has steadily grown in stature with Wolves and has now made his full England debut. Injuries curtailed the start to his Molineux career but he was a star man as they won the Championship. He missed just four games in the season the club returned to the Premier League. The Middlesbrough-born wideman has now signed a contract to stay with Wolves until 2015.

WOLVERHAMPTON WANDERERS

FOUNDED: 1877
GROUND: MOLINEUX
CAPACITY: 29,200
NICKNAME: WOLVES

HONOURS
League Champions:
1954, 1958, 1959
Championship: 2009
Second Division: 1932, 1977
Third Division: 1924, 1989
Fourth Division: 1988
FA Cup: 1893, 1908, 1949, 1960
League Cup: 1974, 1980
League Trophy: 1988

PREMIER LEAGUE
Time in Prem: 2003-04, 09-present
Best finish: 15th (2010)

SEASON 2010-11
Position: 17th
Top scorer: Steven Fletcher, 10
Player of the Season: Matt Jarvis

REMEMBER THIS? Back in 1989 Wolves were promoted as Third Division (League One) Champions – and for the second successive season Steve Bull hit 50 goals. New owner Steve Morgan took over the club in 2007 and promised £30m of investment to get them into the top-flight.

CHAMPIONSHIP
RANGERS RETURN!

QPR were the runaway leaders of the Championship – but at one stage were hit with the threat of a serious points deduction that could have scuppered their promotion hopes.

Rangers were charged by the FA over the signing of Alejandro Faurlin in 2009. They were found guilty of some of the charges and fined £875,000 but escaped losing points.

Rangers returned to the top-flight after an absence of 15 years and it meant that boss Neil Warnock had sealed the seventh promotion of his managerial career.

Norwich City beat their own plans to bounce back to the Premier League within five years thanks to back-to-back promotions.

The 2009-10 League One Champions sealed a return to the top-flight with runner-up spot, climbing into the Premier League – where they were one of the founding members - after an absence of six years.

Swansea City completed their remarkable comeback from almost certain closure to finish third, and then gain Premier League status for the first time by winning the play-off final against Reading.

Cardiff finished fourth but were once again tumbled out of the play-offs having lost the previous season's final.

Reading's fifth-place gained them one of those play-off spots after a remarkable end of season burst of form after they had looked lower table candidates for most of the season.

Low budget Watford slid later in the season to finish 14th, and despite an early season struggle Bristol Rovers climbed to 15th, 18 points clear of danger. Cash-troubled Portsmouth struggled through their crippling financial problems to finish 16th, just ahead of Barnsley, another club operating on a shoestring budget.

Coventry's 18th place and Derby in 19th both left their fans disappointed. But Crystal Palace supporters celebrated the appointment of former striker Dougie Freedman as manager, especially when he helped them escape the pretty tight clutches of relegation.

One place behind the Eagles on goal difference only were Doncaster Rovers, the final team to avoid the bottom three and a trip to League One.

Preston had looked certain for the drop all season and went down as the 22nd-placed side. Sheffield United couldn't snap out of a troubled spell and joined neighbours Wednesday in the third tier, with Scunthorpe who were rock bottom.

Nottingham Forest's high hopes of returning to the Premier League tumbled in the semis, after just scraping into the final play-off spot.

Leeds United, promoted the previous season from League One, looked like they might go straight up to the top-flight but they stuttered when it mattered and were the fastest losers for a play-off place.

Burnley and Millwall were eighth and ninth, not having quite enough in their lockers to mount a challenge for the top six.

Leicester will be fancied for 2011-12 after former England boss Sven Goran Eriksson started to rebuild their side to take the Foxes to a creditable tenth after early season struggles.

Hull were unable to mount serious pressure for a return to the top tier and finished in 11th, just ahead of Middlesbrough who had a remarkable turnaround following the appointment of former player Tony Mowbray as boss.

From looking almost certain relegation candidates, Boro bounced back to 12th.

Another new manager, Paul Jewell, recovered the fortunes of Ipswich Town following the departure of Roy Keane, driving the Tractor Boys up to 13th.

CHAMPIONSHIP FINAL TABLE

		PL	GD	PTS
01	Queens Park Rangers	46	39	88
02	Norwich City	46	25	84
03	Swansea City	46	27	80
04	Cardiff City	46	22	80
05	Reading	46	26	77
06	Nottingham Forest	46	19	75
07	Leeds United	46	11	72
08	Burnley	46	4	68
09	Millwall	46	14	67
10	Leicester City	46	5	67
11	Hull City	46	1	65
12	Middlesbrough	46	0	62
13	Ipswich Town	46	-6	62
14	Watford	46	6	61
15	Bristol City	46	-3	60
16	Portsmouth	46	-7	58
17	Barnsley	46	-11	56
18	Coventry City	46	-4	55
19	Derby County	46	-13	49
20	Crystal Palace	46	-25	48
21	Doncaster Rovers	46	-26	48
22	Preston North End	46	-25	42
23	Sheffield United	46	-35	42
24	Scunthorpe United	46	-44	42

PROMOTION POINTS

QPR keeper Paddy Kenny and midfielder Adel Taarabt were named in the PFA's Championship Team of the Year. Taarabt was also the division's Player of the Year.

The Hoops turned down their local council's plans for a celebration – just like they did seven years earlier after gaining promotion to the Championship.

Rangers were three points away from relegation when Warnock took over as manager in March 2010.

LEAGUE ONE
SEAGULLS FLY HIGH

Brighton were the frontrunners from the start of a frantic season and maintained that position to finish as Champions.

The Seagulls under Gus Poyet were determined and entertaining. The goalscoring exploits of Glenn Murray, a firm defence and a robust midfield ensured their rise to the Championship.

A fantastic run of form from their South Coast neighbours Southampton saw the Saints finish just three points adrift. Nigel Adkins took over the club when they were in 22nd position.

Peterborough made up the third and final side heading to the Championship after one-season back in the third tier. Posh beat Huddersfield Town 3-0 in the play-off final. That was the Terriers first defeat for 23 games, having been one of the top sides all season under Lee Clark.

The surprise package was AFC Bournemouth. The Cherries battled against the departure of two top scorers and a manager to secure a play-off place and get within touching distance of a second successive promotion.

MK Dons took the last play-off place after an impressive season under rookie boss Karl Robinson.

Rochdale, like Bournemouth showed that the promoted teams were no pushovers ending the year in ninth just three points off the play-offs.

Charlton will feel they should have done better with the fourth top scorer in the league, Bradley Wright-Phillips, in their side.

LEAGUE ONE FINAL TABLE

		PL	GD	PTS
01	Brighton & Hove Albion	46	45	95
02	Southampton	46	48	92
03	Huddersfield Town	46	29	87
04	Peterborough United	46	31	79
05	MK Dons	46	7	77
06	AFC Bournemouth	46	21	71
07	Leyton Orient	46	9	70
08	Exeter City	46	-7	70
09	Rochdale	46	8	68
10	Colchester United	46	-6	62
11	Brentford	46	-7	61
12	Carlisle United	46	-2	59
13	Charlton Athletic	46	-4	59
14	Yeovil Town	46	-10	59
15	Sheffield Wednesday	46	0	58
16	Hartlepool United	46	-18	57
17	Oldham Athletic	46	-7	56
18	Tranmere Rovers	46	-7	56
19	Notts County	46	-14	50
20	Walsall	46	-19	48
21	Dagenham & Redbridge	46	-18	47
22	Bristol Rovers	46	-34	45
23	Plymouth Argyle	46	-23	42
24	Swindon Town	46	-22	41

PROMOTION POINTS

After 12 years at the Withdean athletics ground, Brighton started the 2011-12 season at the new 22,500-seat American Express Community Stadium.

More than 15,000 advance season tickets were sold for the Seagulls' return to the Championship.

Liam Bridcutt was without a club at the start of the season after being released by Chelsea. He signed for Brighton, got a new two-year deal and his first-ever goal was voted the club's Goal of the Season!

Swindon completed their remarkable fall from grace, going from play-off finalists to rock bottom in a season. Plymouth were relegated before the final day, paying the price for financial irregularities and a ten point deduction (they would have been safe by five points).

It was final day nerves for Bristol Rovers, Dagenham and Redbridge, Walsall and Notts County. County got the point they needed to secure their League One future, while the Saddlers, beaten at Southampton, had to rely on other results to save them.

LEAGUE TWO
SPIRERITES
MAKE THEIR POINT

Chesterfield, Bury and Wycombe Wanderers are all plying their trade in League One in 2011-12 after sealing the automatic promotion spots from League Two.

Chesterfield went up as deserved champions, the Spirerites fired to the top by the prolific form of strikers Craig Davies and Jack Lester. And boss John Sheridan was handed the PFA League Two Manager of the Year Award.

Bury managed six wins on the bounce to seal second place and Wycombe ensured an immediate return to League One by finishing unbeaten in their final ten games.

PROMOTION POINTS

Chesterfield players Tommy Lee, Danny Whitaker and Craig Davies were named in the PFA League Two team of the Year.

Chesterfield's players weren't the only ones collecting awards – their catering, conference and events teams all collected gongs for their work at the new B2net Stadium.

The £13m B2net Stadium opened its doors on the first day of the 2010-11 campaign with a 2-1 win over Barnet.

LEAGUE TWO FINAL TABLE

		PL	GD	PTS
01	Chesterfield	46	34	86
02	Bury	46	32	81
03	Wycombe Wanderers	46	19	80
04	Shrewsbury Town	46	23	79
05	Accrington Stanley	46	18	73
06	Stevenage Borough	46	17	69
07	Torquay United	46	21	68
08	Gillingham	46	10	68
09	Rotherham United	46	15	66
10	Crewe Alexandra	46	22	65
11	Port Vale	46	5	65
12	Oxford United	46	-2	63
13	Southend United	46	6	61
14	Aldershot Town	46	0	61
15	Macclesfield Town	46	-15	55
16	Northampton Town	46	-8	52
17	Cheltenham Town	46	-21	52
18	Bradford City	46	-25	52
19	Burton Albion	46	-14	51
20	Morecambe	46	-19	51
21	Hereford United	46	-16	50
22	Barnet	46	-19	48
23	Lincoln City	46	-36	47
24	Stockport County	46	-48	41

Stevenage sealed back-to-back promotions after victory in the play-off final against Torquay United.

Stockport County finished bottom and suffered a second successive relegation. They were joined in the Blue Square Premier by Lincoln City who were relegated on the last day.

Disappointing campaigns from the previous season's other relegated sides, saw Gillingham just miss out on a play-off place and mid-table mediocrity for Southend United.

Oxford United completed their return to the League with a steady but impressive 12th place finish, in what was a tight end to the season.

Anyone from 14th upwards could have sneaked into the play-offs. It was Accrington Stanley and Shrewsbury Town that joined Stevenage and Torquay but fell at the first hurdle.

Much was expected of Rotherham, and star man Adam Le Fondre, but the Millers stuttered to ninth. Free-scoring Crewe managed a better goal difference than most above them but were tenth.

The mix up at the bottom saw many clubs battling against the drop. Northampton and Cheltenham Towns secured safety early, as did Bradford City. Burton Albion and Morecambe left it late, and Hereford were all but safe barring an unprecedented set of final results on the last day.

MAD MASCOTS!

Don't you just love those crazy characters and furry beasts that act as mascots for football teams? Some have proved to be madder than others…

SWANNING ABOUT

You don't mess with Cyril the Swan! He's a real top bird! The mascot of Premier League new boys Swansea City has been involved in fights with other mascots and stewards and even appeared in court for his bad behaviour. Cyril has starred in pantomime, has his own replica soft toys, been fined and been in big bother for leading a pitch invasion!

INFAMOUS FOR: Ripping the head off Millwall's Zampa the Lion and kicking it along the ground.

MONKEY BUSINESS

One of the most famous mascots around is H'Angus Monkey, mascot to Hartlepool, favourite side of Sky Sports presenter Jeff Stelling. The monkey outfit relates to when one of the primates was found on the local beach during the First World War and was hanged as a spy. The monkey suit was once worn by Stuart Drummond, later to become the town's Mayor after running with a campaign to offer free bananas to school children!

INFAMOUS FOR: Being ejected from the ground for leading fans in a singsong.

BEE STING

Bertie Bee proved that despite his nice furry appearance he carries quite a sting! When a streaker ran across the pitch during his Burnley side's match against Preston, Bertie buzzed into action. As the naked man avoided capture by stewards, Bertie ran into the streaker's path and then upped him over his shoulder and sent him flat on the ground.

INFAMOUS FOR: Doing a weird butterfly swimming stroke along the touchline after nabbing the streaker.

YOU'RE OFF!

Reading's Kingsley Lion was sent-off by referee Mike Riley! The man in black reckoned that the mascot in the blue and white hooped shirt was confusing him. Kingsley has also been sent-off for a handball and was once flattened by Royals' captain Graeme Murty, a fight which left the mascot without a head!

INFAMOUS FOR: Manager Steve Coppell's quote after the mascot was sent off: "He does look like so many of my players."

DRAGON'S DEN

Rochdale's Desmond Dragon wasn't happy when he saw Freddie Fox of Halifax cock his leg up against his side's goal post. Freddie had pulled Desmond's tail earlier and been pushed backwards into the goal before cocking his leg.

INFAMOUS FOR: Being ejected by the police for the above incident.

Match up the Mascot

Do you know which beast backs which club? Here are five mascots and five club badges for you to match up. Answers page 78.

Gunnersaurus

Elephant

Lofty the Lion

Moonbeam

Roary the Tiger

Everton

Bolton

Arsenal

Hull City

Man City

The hair restorer sold to Newcastle fans made them all look like defender Fabricio Coloccini

Shay Given decides it's time he got in some training for Strictly Come Dancing.

Stoke City suffer a severe shortage of supporters...

FUNNY OLD GAME

Our photographers have snapped some great shots at games over the past year...

HERE ARE JUST A FEW

THE GENERATION GAME

DAVID WEIR

Date of birth: May 10, 1970
Debut: 1986, Evansville University, USA
Total club games: 749+ and counting
International: Scotland (69 caps, 1 goal)

Incredibly, central defender Weir didn't join Scottish giants Rangers until the age of 37 having playing for Falkirk, Hearts and Everton. He played his first game for Scotland in 1997, retired from international duty in 2002, but then returned in August 2010 at the age of 40!

RYAN GIGGS

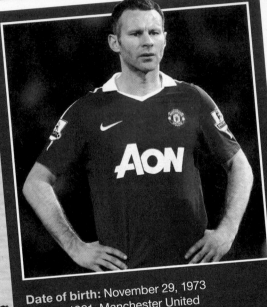

Date of birth: November 29, 1973
Debut: 1991, Manchester United
Total club games: 870+ and counting
International: Wales (64 caps, 12 goals)

Giggs retired from international football in 2007 to concentrate on his club career – and what a smart move that was! Still playing and influencing games after his 37th birthday, midfielder Giggsy is one of the best players of his time with 12 Premier League titles and four FA Cups to his credit.

STEVE HARPER

Date of birth: March 14, 1975
Debut: 1995, Huddersfield
Total club games: 245+ and counting
International: N/A

Newcastle keeper Harper would have made more appearances if he hadn't remained loyal to the Magpies and understudy to Shay Given for many years. Loaned to five clubs before making his United debut in 1999. Took the No.1 shirt at St. James' Park following Given's departure to Man City.

SOME PLAYERS APPEAR TO HAVE BEEN AROUND FOREVER!

Better lifestyles and improved training methods have given many stars longer on the pitch than they could have expected. Here are a few who have proved there is life well after the age of 30...

EXTRA TIME: Welshman Gary Speed was the first player to play 500 games in the Premier League. When he retired in 2010 the midfielder had totalled 831 appearances for Leeds, Newcastle, Everton, Bolton and Sheffield United in the top two tiers.

PAUL SCHOLES

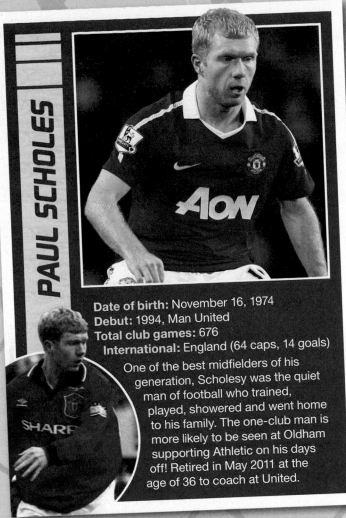

Date of birth: November 16, 1974
Debut: 1994, Man United
Total club games: 676
International: England (64 caps, 14 goals)

One of the best midfielders of his generation, Scholesy was the quiet man of football who trained, played, showered and went home to his family. The one-club man is more likely to be seen at Oldham supporting Athletic on his days off! Retired in May 2011 at the age of 36 to coach at United.

BRAD FRIEDEL

Date of birth: May 18, 1971
Debut: 1995, Galatasaray
Total club games: 601+ and counting
International: USA (82 caps, 0 goals)

The keeper has played for Liverpool, Blackburn, Aston Villa and Spurs – even notching a goal during his time with Rovers! The reliable shot-stopper set a record when he appeared in 250 consecutive Premier League appearances. Man of the Match in Rovers' League Cup win over Tottenham in 2002.

KEVIN PHILLIPS

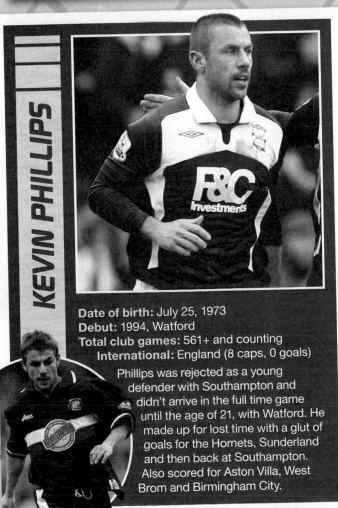

Date of birth: July 25, 1973
Debut: 1994, Watford
Total club games: 561+ and counting
International: England (8 caps, 0 goals)

Phillips was rejected as a young defender with Southampton and didn't arrive in the full time game until the age of 21, with Watford. He made up for lost time with a glut of goals for the Hornets, Sunderland and then back at Southampton. Also scored for Aston Villa, West Brom and Birmingham City.

DAVID BECKHAM

Date of birth: May 2, 1975
Debut: 1992, Man United
Total club games: 650+ and counting
International: England (115 caps, 17 goals)

There's not a football fan on the planet who hasn't heard of Becks! His career at Man United, Real Madrid, LA Galaxy and spells on loan at AC Milan have ensured a place in history for the boy from the East End. England's most-capped outfield player with a sweet right foot!

THEY LOVE ROO!

Wayne Rooney's love affair with Manchester United looked over when he asked for a transfer at the start of season 2010-11. He claimed he hadn't really wanted to leave – and the result was a whacking big new contract. And for the rest of the season he did his best to win back the support of Red Devils' fans...

DID YOU REALLY WANT TO LEAVE?

"I made a mistake. When I look back at it now, I'll say it again, how wrong was I? I'm willing to admit that. I've apologised and ever since then I have wanted to try to prove myself again to the fans. I'm a lot happier in my life, a lot happier with the way I'm playing."

YOU'RE AT UNITED FOR A WHILE THEN?

"I'm signed here until I am 30 now, so I'm hoping I can stay here. I doubt I can do what Scholesy and Giggs have done because I don't think I have the right body to play so long. I've changed the way I live my life, I've started doing my coaching badges and I'd like to be a manager one day."

YOU FANCY BEING A BOSS?

"There are a lot of ex-United players who have played under Sir Alex who have gone on to become good managers and I'm hoping I can do that. But I wouldn't like to follow this manager. I'd rather start by going down and learning something about the lower leagues. I don't think it's fair if a manager gets a big job with no experience."

SO TELL US ABOUT SIR ALEX...

"There are days when I don't want to see the manager, he can be fierce at times. Even after we've won 2-0 or 3-0, and the lads are laughing thinking we have played well, he can sometimes come in and let loose. Our dressing room is not a nice place to be when we lose – he is a perfectionist!"

EXTRA TIME: Wayne and his wife Coleen love dogs, and their pets have included Bichon Frisés, a chow and a French mastiff. The pooches live in luxury with specially built and heated kennels at the couple's home in Cheshire

WAYNE MARK ROONEY
Position: Striker
Birth date: October 24, 1985
Birth place: Croxteth, Liverpool
Height: 1.78m (5ft 10in)
Clubs: Everton, Manchester United
International: England

DO YOU EVER THINK ABOUT GETTING INJURED?

"You can't worry about going into a game and getting injured. There's nothing you can do about it, you have just got to accept it. Occasionally you will try to get out of the way of a tackle and it looks like a dive. You can tell when people dive to win a free-kick and it is up to the ref to deal with it."

AND WHAT ABOUT OFF THE PITCH?

"You are role models whether you like it or not, so you need to do your best on the pitch and do things well for kids to see. It is very rare now that I would go to a nightclub."

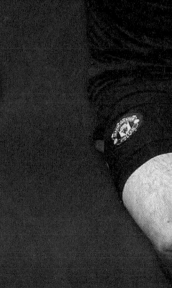

WERE YOU EVER SERIOUSLY GOING TO LEAVE OLD TRAFFORD?

"I don't really like to go down to London, I am a northern lad. Could you ever see me playing for a foreign team? No! I love England and I love being close to the family."

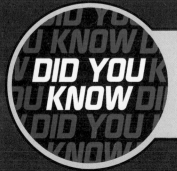

DID YOU KNOW

Wayne's younger brother, John, played for Macclesfield and in America's MLS. Their older cousin, Tommy, was also on the books at Macc before going into non-league football. Another older cousin, James, a wannabee pop singer, made an attempt to get onto X Factor.

EXTRA TIME: The Rooneys like a nice meal and have been spotted at their local Gusto Italian restaurant and picking up a Chinese from a takeaway not far from their home. Wayne's also partial to lasagne, spaghetti and chicken dishes.

SHOOT ANNUAL 2012 **73**

TOP TRIVIA

The good, the bad and the ridiculous from the sometimes weird world of football!

SHOOTING STAR

Chelsea player Ashley Cole notched up a load of YouTube hits when he appeared as… a cartoon character!

Following the alleged incident when the England defender took a gun into the Blues training ground, Taiwan animators had a field day. They had Cole dressed as a jester firing the gun in the changing rooms – and in less than two weeks the film attracted more than 500,000 hits.

NUTS!

Dimitar Berbatov has been driven nuts!

But it's not by the antics of Manchester United's Wayne Rooney or due to any missed chances in front of goal.

The former Bulgaria striker became a target for a plague of squirrels. Berba used to throw nuts to squirrels from the balcony on his London home when he was a Tottenham.

And in Manchester he also started to feed the furry rodents but then hordes of them arrived in his garden!

TAKE ME TO THE MOON!

Striker Mario Balotelli is a big star in Italy – and he's been checking out a few more in Manchester.

But the hitman isn't admiring his City team-mates or even the big guns at United… he's hooked on astronomy!

The unpredictable frontman has a telescope which he uses on the balcony of his penthouse home to keep an eye on the stars and planets!

RED RECORD

A referee set a new world record when he sent off 36 players during a football game in Argentina in 2011!

OFF went all 22 players. OFF went the substitutes as well following a mass brawl as Claypole played Victoriano Arenas.

The previous record for dismissals was 20, during a game in Paraguay.

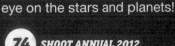

LIVERPOOL GET THE BEAT

Bet you all thought Liverpool's improved form in the second half of season 2010-11 was down to the return of legend Kenny Dalglish.

Well he might have had something to do with it, but striker Dirk Kuyt reckons he is the man who tuned up the Reds… with his iPod!

"Ever since I plugged my iPod into our music system and played my stuff we started winning," he said. Music for success? Kings of Leon, The Killers and Amy Winehouse. What, no Beatles?

DEADLY RIVALS

British club chairmen and players who think they get a rough ride from fans should listen to what happened in Guatemala.

The vice president of struggling Deportivo Xinabajul, in the country's top-flight, was ambushed and shot dead after he received threats from disgruntled supporters.

And just a few months earlier a player with a club in the country's second division was found murdered after accusations he had affairs with women.

GOOD SPORTS

Don't get involved in taking on winger Matt Jarvis at any sports! You are likely to get a hammering!

When he was younger, the Wolves wideman was Surrey breastroke champion and ran cross country for England, and was a bit handy at the 800m and 1,500mm.

His parents, Nick and Linda, were rated No.1 in the country at table tennis – so he's probably a bit good at that too!

There could be problems at home over football! Dad follows home town team Middlesbrough; Matt, brother Ben and mum are self-confessed Manchester United followers!

QUICK HITS

England striker Wayne Rooney has become a big fan of Thomas the Tank Engine. His Man United team-mates reckon he's an expert since he started reading books to son Kai and watching the train on DVD.

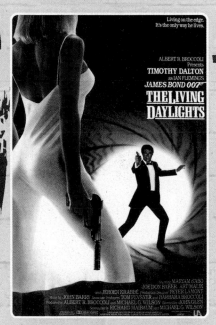

Former James Bond, Timothy Dalton, has admitted he's been a Manchester City fan since the age of 8. Now in his late 60s, secret agent 007 says he used to sneak into former ground Maine Road without paying!

The average football fan clocks up an estimated 2,000 miles a year following a team. A survey reckoned that West Brom followers were the long-distance experts with an average of 3,290 miles and Blackburn the short runners at 1,312 miles.

WHAT'S HAPPENED HERE?

TWO PICTURES FROM TWO BIG GAMES – and we've let our designer get to work on them both to make six changes to each. All you have to do is be more eagle-eyed than the best referee around and see if you can Spot the Differences! Draw rings around the differences in pictures A and B.

EXTRA TIME: Viktor Kassai, the referee for the Man United v Barcelona Champions League Final in 2011, was the youngest man in black to officiate in this fixture. The Hungarian was 35 and beat by four years the previous best set by Pierluigi Collina.

A

B

EXTRA TIME: Striker Grant Holt has played his way from non-League, through all of the lower Football Leagues, to Premier League in just ten years. He was Norwich City's top-scorer as they were promoted from the Championship in May 2011.

SHOOT ANNUAL 2012 77

ALL THE ANSWERS

Page 10 FAMOUS FACES
1963 Sir Alex Ferguson
1979 Phil Thompson
1980 Sam Allardyce
1984 (a) Gary Lineker
1984 (b) Steve Bruce
1992 (a) Jamie Redknapp
1992 (b) Alan Shearer
1997 Paul Jewell and Chris Kamara

Page 12 QUIZ Part One
01. Marouane Chamakh
02. Ivory Coast
03. £50m
04. Real Madrid
05. Two from:
     Tottenham, West Ham, Fulham
06. Ghana
07. He scored their first-ever World
     Cup finals goals in 2006.
08. Charlton
09. Feyenoord
10. Bulgarian
11. French
12. Brazil

Page 14 SPOT THE SCOUT

Page 22 QUIZ Part Two
01. Southampton
02. Barcelona
03. Potters
04. Arsenal, Emirates Stadium
05. Nottingham Forest
06. Real Madrid
07. Liverpool
08. Chelsea
09. Tottenham
10. Newcastle and Notts County
11. Swansea
12. Derby

Page 28 NAME THAT PLAYER
A. Tim Cahill
B. Javier Hernandez (Little Pea)
C. Luis Suarez
D. Aaron Ramsey

**Page 29
CHAMPIONSHIP CHALLENGE**
A. Middlesbrough (Boro)
B. Swansea (Swans)
C. Portsmouth (Pompey)
D. Leeds United (The Whites)
E. Nottingham Forest
     (Forest or The Reds)
F. Bristol City (Robins)

Page 34 QUIZ Part Three
01. Holland
02. Andres Iniesta
03. Fernando Torres
04. 3-3
05. Didier Drogba
06. Michael Owen
07. Jermain Defoe
08. True
09. Manchester United
10. Kenny Dalglish
11. Arsenal
12. Ashley Young

Page 39 WHICH BALL
GAME 1: F
GAME 2: D
GAME 3: D
GAME 4: B

Page 42 QUIZ Part Four
01. Italy
02. Blackburn Rovers
03. Twice
04. 17
05. True
06. Peru
07. Ashley Cole
08. 10
09. All play for Ivory Coast
10. Bournemouth
11. Chesterfield
12. Neil Warnock

Page 45 THEY SAID WHAT
A. Wenger
B. Mourinho
C. Redknapp
D. Ferguson
E. Keegan
F. Cantona

Page 67 MASCOTS
Gunnersaurus - Arsenal
Elephant - Everton
Lofty the Lion - Bolton
Moonbeam - Man City
Roary the Tiger - Hull City

**Page 68
SPOT THE DIFFERENCE**